Inclusive Data

How Making Almighty Data Cavityism History Can Update The Future

Aaron W. Wemple

Life Winks LLC

CONTENTS

Dedication

Dedicated to our community, volunteers and partners.

Some will view it as a harmful, sick, or unsustainable pairing. But all-natural, special-needs data fields and the systemic production of profitable data should live in harmony.

This book is dedicated to the selfless ReboundHeros who continue to fight for justice and equality. Helping those who are typically disadvantaged or lack resources achieve their goals. Together, they're making an incredible, awe-inspiring contribution to the future of data for content lovers everywhere with ground-breaking innovations and often invisible stakes on the front lines transformed lives.

This book is dedicated to the volunteers and partners who have contributed to making Inclusive Data a reality. These individuals have given their time and energy to help make our project a success. We are sincerely grateful for their support.

It's like we're investing in organic farmers who are innovating new ways to increase crop yields and profitability. Heroes are betting on them to create new value and new wealth for society.

Lastly, we dedicate it to organic representatives for innovative types of data profiteering metrics, new data value and new data "storage" methods that their vulnerable members have transformed circumstances to be more functional, profitable, and easily available.

Because advocating Inclusive Data will come across toxic, it nonetheless still offers numerous advantages over unpaired traditional data metrics, value and storage protocols, including instantaneous access times, no barriers for data floods in the line, in-home best security, and not just no costs, but reverse costs form what the digital floods are used too. It's dedicated to unsung heroes leading others to hidden treasure troves.

Thanks to them, there are no barriers to entry, the security is top-notch, and the rewards are plentiful. So for saving our future struggles and information, this book is for you!

Introduction

The past of going data rates: Exclusive. It's like trying to get from New York to Los Angeles in a car with no gas pedal.

Inclusive Data deals are like a gas pedal and always there when you need it. Making organic data exchangeable and more accessible to all. Which is not currently a viable access and search engine deal. The bodies of a once-great internet stack up, its algorithms long forgotten, its protocol interfaces a mockery of its former glory. It now exists only against those with circumstantial, intellectual and physical barriers in life.

INCLUSIVE DATA

In this book, you'll read about a woman named Amy who discovers that her entire life has been a lie when she tries to download her memories and finds that her data rate has been deliberately restricted. A man nicknamed Daredevil Dan who finds himself unable to connect to the internet or any digital devices as he and the world believes. And Angel Ang who moves the unlikely team into a new data garden, only to discover that their interface is uncomfortably different. They soon realize that the previous occupants of data were brutally profitable, and that their ghosts are haunting the weak and dragging down the data rates.

The term "data" refers to information that has been collected and analyzed. "Pure" data is data that has not been altered in any way. "Unadulterated" data is data that has not been tampered with or manipulated in any way. "Set systems" are systems in which data is collected and stored. We know that data that comes from set systems is not always pure or unadulterated.

Even though data that is pure and unadulterated is best, we know that data that comes from set systems has its way. Especially when socioeconomics are at play.

When discussing data, it is important to keep in mind that "pure" data (data that has not been tampered with in any way) is often not possible to obtain. In many cases, the best we can hope for is data that comes from a set system plus some interpretation assistance - a system and assist where the data has been collected in a systematic way and where there is some level of personal quality control.

Data Cavityism is the term used to describe the tendency of data sets to only include information that supports pre-existing narratives and ignore anything that doesn't fit into that narrative. This means that data sets are often biased and don't give an accurate representation of reality. Data has always been exclusionary. In order to make data more inclusive, we need to understand how data has always been exclusionary, and then help Data has always been exclusionary. In order to make data more inclusive, we need help to undergo "transformation." For example, a study on income inequality might only look at data from wealthy countries, which would give a misleading picture of global inequality.

The study of income and expenses for corporate boards will look at data differently than for families or children. For example, a corporate board may be interested in looking at the total income for the company, while a family may be interested in looking at their monthly expenses.

The study of income and expense data is important for both corporate boards and families or children because it helps them understand where their money is coming from and where it is going. For example, a corporate board might want to know how much money the company is making and where all of the expenses will be designated to go. A family or child might want to know how much money they have to spend on things like food, clothes, and toys. Yet, both have different capacities to guide community data.

Inclusive Data is a critical part of understanding the world and making decisions, but it has historically been difficult for underrepresented groups to access. This is starting to change, as organizations are beginning to realize the new value of inclusive data. By making data more accessible and understandable, we can update the future.

In a civilized society, it should be against the law to keep certain types of information away from people based on how much money they have. This is because everyone deserves an equal chance to succeed, and withholding information unfairly gives some people an advantage over others. Imagine if only rich kids were allowed to go to school while poor kids had to work instead. That would be very unfair, and it would be hard for the poor kids to catch up. Helping access or "ramp" Inclusive Data access equally is a start.

INCLUSIVE DATA

In a world where big-Big data is becoming increasingly more accessible, it's hard to believe that there are still people being denied this information. It's even harder to believe that this is happening in developed countries. Surely in a civilized society, everyone should have access to data care?

There are many reasons why people may not have access to data. It could be because they can't afford it, or because it's not available in their language. But whatever the reason, denying people access to data is tantamount to denying them a voice.

If we want to create a fairer, more inclusive society, then we need to make sure that everyone has access to data. It's not enough to just make data available – it needs to be affordable and easy to understand too. Otherwise, we're just creating another form of big-Bigger inequality.

There are many reasons why data sets are often exclusionary - they don't care. However, reading on proves you're an inclusionary, a treasure hunting visionary like ReboundHeros. Like putting a gas pedal in every car for every trip.

The future: Inclusive Data.

Blurbs

Blurbs

"I just want to give a shout out to my friend Aaron Wemple. He helps people going through the family court system. He never gives up despite having little resources and few supporters. He's been a blessing to me and supported me until I finally got access to my children. I love you brother!"

-Author Denis Durham

"One of my favorite authors. This work, I know, is about creating data more accessibly that includes everyone. Something I know Mr. Wemple has dedicated his life to."

-Dr. Sinha

"The safety file invention by Aaron Wemple help restore my life and the lives of many people. It was a game changer and saves countless lives during their worse and most excluding deal-makings imaginable."

-Founder Olivia Sanders

-

Chapter 1

Faith and Freedom Vs. Binding Deals

Do you struggle with this?

My favorite part of waking up in the morning is watching the sky transition from dark to light. It's like a big painting that gradually becomes more and more colorful as the sun rises. I'm always eager to see the first glimpse of light in the distance. Its effects are wondrous and unpredictable, like the workings of divine faith in Jesus. A valuable feeling added to my physiology of pure bliss and joy every moment of every day.

But when I get up and walk into the bathroom, I face a dilemma. It's the first of many problems to be solved that I'll be dealing with today. Do I stay faithful to my convictions and remain free, or do I give in to temptation and bind myself to the chains of a power bill by flipping the light switch? Do I stay socioeconomically safe and risk my morning bathroom routine in the dark, or do I pay attention to details about what I'm doing and feel more secure?

Could you imagine not having access to both sunlight and socioeconomic abilities of deciding free versus paid-light because of physical limitations like blindness? As scary as it may sound, some people have to endure this frightening reality. They live in complete darkness, unable to see or experience anything outside their homes. They're completely alone, at best. At worst, they're not "talked with," they're "talked at." It's like being in a dark room, with someone standing over you and shouting at you. You can't understand them or why their ego's growing, but you can't escape it no matter how isolated you become.

When Molly Burke was four years old, she began losing her vision. By the time she was 14, she was completely blind. Despite her blindness, Molly has achieved amazing things. She is a motivational speaker and influencer (Burke, 2018).

Molly's story is one of hope and inspiration. When she was first diagnosed with an eye condition that would eventually lead to her blindness, Molly's parents were told that their daughter would never be able to live a "normal" life. But Molly proved them wrong.

Recently, Molly said in an inspiring YouTube video, "Some put their lives in other's hands, I put mine in the paws of a dog."

In her talks and interviews, Molly likes to remind people that anything is possible if you set your mind to it. In the video, Molly swallows intently and then starts to explain her debilitating story by saying, "I'm about to tell a story I have never told before. I am a YouTuber and a motivational speaker, and I happen to be blind. I was born with a rare genetic eye disease called retinitis pigmentosa, which is the deterioration of your retina. When I was little, I could see and then as I slowly grew up, my vision actually caved in. And by grade 4, I had to start using my white cane full time."

What it is like to go blind

It's hard to imagine what it would be like to go blind. For most of us, our vision is something we take for granted. But for Molly Burke, losing her sight was very real and debilitated the world around her.

"Even at such a young age," Molly went on to say in her interview, "I realized the stigma that surrounded that. I realized nobody is ever going to come up to me and be like, 'How old is your cane?' 'What's its name?'" Molly seemed to sense that nothing would ever be straight forward again.

Molly then moved on to explain to her audience triumphantly, "But I knew that if I had a dog, it would break down that barrier again. Instead of being the weird girl with a cane, I'd be the cool girl with the dog in school, and everybody would actually want to talk to me - would want to learn."

As her condition progressively became worse, Molly became increasingly reliant on her other senses and special needs assistance providers. She learned to use tactile cues and where to find outside assistance like the dog she dreamed about to better access her world.

She went alone on the six-hour train ride when she was only 13 years old. The train ride would take her from English-speaking Ontario to French-speaking Quebec. Where she would spend the next 4 weeks of her life at a guide-dog school. Molly describes her experiences, "I was the youngest in training that month by almost 10 years. And she was the only non-French speaker. It was a very isolating and lonely experience having no one to talk to except my new guide dog, and she (the dog) was not very good at holding conversation (Burke, 2018)."

As Molly became more aware of her vision loss, she said that she felt like she had to stuff those feelings in order to maintain the scary task at hand of getting to use a comfort pet. She said sadly, "Over the course of the month of training, my vision became worse and worse. Black (colors) started looking Gray. Yellow started looking White. Everything was just fading away, but my trust in my dog became better and better. And my confidence became stronger and stronger with my first guide dog Gypsy.

Sadly, Molly went on, "Gypsy passed away about 4 years ago. It was the most devastating thing I've been through next to my vision loss itself, but one of the things you have to accept when you become a service dog user and you spend 24 hours a day with an animal you put your trust and your life into them it is so much more than losing a pet, it's like losing a limb and it's really, really hard."

Her second guide dog's name is Gallup. She feels like Gallup teaches her to slow down and relax. To take a breath and take some time for herself. To lower her heart rate whenever she gets anxious or stressed (Burke, 2018).

Molly ended her incredible story by saying, "I know that every dog that comes into my life is with me to teach me a certain lesson. And although it's only been two (dogs) at this point, I know it's going to continue on. The incredible time that you have with them, and what they bring to your life, is so worth it!

"What I learned that month," Molly says, "is that sometimes walking into a dark and scary situation can actually lead you to find the light" (Burke, 2018).

Read on to discover where people who have gone from blindness to being able to see have found the light.

Chapter 2

Faith and Freedom Vs. Newly Free Data Access

My favorite part of waking up in the morning is watching the sky transition from dark to light. Like most people, my routine in the morning has become almost clear. I flip a switch after getting up and pay for light—a luxury decision that isn't available to everyone. Some people require a comfort dog or a sense of a comforting routine to navigate their steps through life. Even better, they thrive regardless of my ignorance!

In the New Yorker, Dr. Pawan Sinha, an eye surgeon who is also a professor of vision and computational neuroscience at M.I.T., wanted to know what people who became cured of blindness could see compared to what they thought before they were cured when they couldn't according to House, 2014. It was an age-old debate, one that had been around for centuries. It was a debate that people were passionate about, one that lingered and often led to professional missteps.

The philosopher William Molyneux, whose wife was blind, proposed a thought experiment in 1688 about a person blind from birth who could tell the difference between a cube and a sphere by touch: If her vision were restored and she was presented with the same cube and sphere, would she be able to tell which was which by sight alone? The philosophical problem divided camps through the centuries into those who believe that certain qualities are innate and shared among the senses (the Yes camp), and those who insist that, to understand roundness, the eyes must have already seen roundness (the No camp). After the discovery in 1747 that a simple cataract surgery could lift the curtain of blindness for some people, Molyneux's thought experiment simply became an experiment.

Just a New "Interface?"

Dr. Sinha, through a non-profit organization he established called Project Prakash, has donated sight-restoration surgeries to more than 200 blind children from impoverished regions of India. The surgeries were given to any child who medically qualified, a subset of whom had been blind since birth with cataracts. After sight had been restored, Sinha posed Molyneux's question (House, 2014).

The consequences would have likely disillusioned the ones in Molyneux's Yes camp. Sinha recorded a video where a teen-age boy, blind from birth due to opaque cataracts, sees for the first time. The boy sits silently and blinks, his eyes reflecting light from around the room as they adjust after years of darkness. Sinha believes those first moments are blurry, incoherent and saturated with colors that don't make sense as shapes or faces or any type of object. "The moments right now following bandage removal aren't as `magical` as Hollywood films might have us believe," Sinha advised me. To answer Molyneux: No; a cube and a sphere are misunderstood in this confusion .

Just a new "interface" for accessibility? No way! This is a complete overhaul of the user experience, designed to make life easier and more productive, but also a new "interface" issue that couldn't have been known systemically.

New "Accessabilities" in Data Are Not New Interfaces for Users with Special Needs

Vision researcher and psychologist Stephen Kosslyn told Dr. Sinha that he was not surprised by the results of the study. A few of the apparently innate traits in regular vision, he said, are actually learned through experience. He provided an example of stereoscopic vision, which requires the eyes to combine two barely similar images into a single sharp perception. "In order for stereoscopic vision to work," he said, "the mind must know something about how far apart the eyes are." Factors like prenatal nutrition can affect bone growth, which can set the eyes at varying distances from each other. "The mind cannot probably know this before being born," he said; and so, in those first moments of new sight—even with two good eyes—the incoming light will be mishandled by unprepared psychology (House, 2014).

In 1993, Dr. Pawan Sinha published an article on how quickly, if at all, the brain acceptability and vision return after surgery. It depends entirely on the circumstance. Oliver Sacks wrote a story in the magazine about Virgil, a man with limited to no vision as a child who had developed cataracts at the age of six. After his cataracts were removed, fifty years later, Virgil had trouble adjusting. (For example, he could not always distinguish the letter "A" from the letter "H" and when given Molyneux's test could not tell a square he felt from a square he saw.)

If people with special needs suddenly saw the sun rising and could decide whether or not to turn on the bathroom light, would they then have light and data inclusivity?

Following the surgery, Sinha checked in with the Prakash children and found that many higher-order aspects of vision were improving. In a few months, they could match felt objects to their visual counterparts, and they improved at spatial-navigation tasks requiring mental imagery. The finding was particularly important because previous work by Kosslyn and others had found that the congenitally blind have a capacity for mental imagery, but it is limited in some ways and becomes increasingly poor as the task becomes more complex. (In one example, a sighted person will imagine a typewriter a few feet away as larger than the same one imagined a hundred feet away.

Among the congenitally blind, however, the imagined typewriter—a composite of experiences of touch and sound alone—is the same size at all distances.)

Kosslyn believes that "When you develop expectations, you can use the fruits of previous experience to help you process what's coming in now," Kosslyn said. "You need to have had that experience" (House, 2014).

People who are cured of being paralyzed see walking differently than those who have never been paralyzed (Poncumhak et al., 2014). That is according to a new study published in the journal Frontiers in Human Neuroscience. The findings suggest that our brains adapt to our physical abilities and expectations of what we can do, said lead author Dr. Phillippe Goldin, an associate professor of psychiatry at Stanford University School of Medicine.

"Our study shows that even after people recover from spinal cord injury, they continue to think about walking in ways that conform to their current level of function," Goldin said online.

People with spinal cord injuries often describe a shift in perspective on what it means to walk after regaining mobility, he added.

"They say that when they had no hope of recovery, they thought about walking in terms of movement and coordination," Goldin said. "After recovery, however, some say that now the act of walking feels more like a social experience" (Poncumhak et al., 2014).

The researchers studied 29 people with spinal cord injuries who had regained partial use of their legs between six months and two years earlier and 20 healthy adults without any impairments in motor function or mobility. Each participant was asked to imagine themselves walking forward around obstacles such as trees or lampposts and then again without them. The researchers concluded that these changes in how people with spinal cord injuries perceive space may help explain why some people find it difficult to navigate certain environments after an injury — even if they can walk independently again.

"What if data is always flooding and never organically produced?"

The Data Ramp "Interface" Application Process

An implied paradox of "inclusivity" data exists between those with special needs and those without. An insight known as the "Inclusivity Paradox" demonstrates how individuals with disabilities commonly fare compared to those without disabilities. Like endless and ongoing backwards "access."

Therefore, Inclusive Data previously unregistered must start out as a presumed "interface" issue for a periodically publicly accessible time. Like turning backwards data "access" into propped-up Open Access. It's theorized that bound data, what we commonly think of as big data flood waters, and newly free data access, what we commonly think of as access ramps for routine life rescues, informational searches and actionable steps, are both lost in the confusing interface between those with special needs and those without special needs. Even better, people thrive regardless of other people's ignorance!

"Yeah, it can be a pain, but everything twins greatness anyway."

It's Required

If you were in a wheelchair and needed help getting around, would you want someone to help you or install a ramp? Of course you would! The same goes for if you have special access requirements and challenges when browsing the internet. You need Inclusive Data care!

Chapter 3

Exclusive Data's Future Rise

What is exclusive data and its advantages?

Exclusive data is a term for inorganic data but can only be accessible by a certain group of people. A VIP room in a club is exclusive because it can only be accessed by a certain group of people. This type of data has many advantages, including the ability to make better decisions, avoid competition, and gain insights that would otherwise be unavailable.

One of the main advantages of exclusive data is that it allows companies to make better decisions for the bottom-line. With access to manipulation with information that others don't have, businesses can gain a competitive edge and make choices that are based on more than just guesswork. Additionally, having exclusive data can help companies avoid competition. If other businesses don't have the same information, they may be at a disadvantage when trying to compete. Finally, gaining insights from exclusive data can help businesses improve their products or services. By understanding what customers want and need, companies can make changes that will be well-received and improve their bottom line. It's like when you're trying a new recipe for the first time. You can always adjust the ingredients to suit your taste.

Have you ever been in a college class when the teacher asked a question? And you knew the answer so you raised your hand high. You turn and look around. No one else is raising their hand. So, you get a little more excited. But the teacher never calls on you. Yet, this is the last question of the semester. The final chance for some extra credit you need to pass before the final decision is made, and the grade is in the record books forever. One moment in time to either propel your life forward or else get held back and prevent you from moving forward. The teacher never calls you. And since you didn't get a voice, your whole future doesn't advance as you dreamed. (That's Academic Cavityism caused by exclusivity).

Now, imagine that you're a child like my friend Olivia was in the 2nd grade. Her mom came home and she was that good student who sacrificed everything and knew the right answer. Normally, she said, when her mom walked through the door, she was happy. But that day, she was inconsolable and sad. In the following days, she watched her mom start boxing up clothes to move. Soon after, the car disappeared. The house was taken. There was no money for food or a new place to live. Even her dog was gone. (That's pet Cavityism, where Olivia's physiology felt and forever knew the absence of being rejected.)

Turns out, it wasn't a college class at all. That was a family court. And the disenfranchiser wasn't the teacher. That was a judge and the final ruling. You see, her mom couldn't afford an expensive retainer fee for representation. But her opponent could afford a whole team of lawyers. (Disclaimer: some states do try providing representation disparity relief, but that's not effective when parties live outside each other's jurisdictions). That's why my company and its partners must become a resource that the community can tap into for representational disparity relief and Inclusive Data restorations.

Together, we're like a safety net for kids, those with special needs, and family sustainability when other paths can't. Different partnerships for different purposes. We'll save lives, prevent unnecessary trauma, and provide fair and inclusive life advancement. Oh, and preventing missing dogs too.

So that someday when someone you love is sitting in a classroom and has the right answer, raising their hand high with excitement, preparing for the next phase in their life, they won't have to let down. You'll know safer alternatives like constructive child safety files and a fairer voice before it's too late.

The future of exclusive data: what to expect

The future of exclusive data is looking very bright. With the ever-growing amount of big data being produced, it is becoming increasingly important to have a way to store and manage it all. Exclusive Data is one such focus that is rising to the challenge. It'll offer a variety of services, like more secure "access," that will be designed to help businesses make the most of their data. From storage and backup to analytics and consulting, Exclusive Data is poised to help profitable businesses take advantage of the big data revolution.

It's a rapidly developing world, and data is becoming increasingly important. So as our reliance on technology as a society grows, so does the importance of data. The future rise of exclusive data refers to the trend of businesses and organizations collecting and using data that is not available to their competitors. This allows them to gain a competitive advantage and be more efficient and effective in their operations.

There are many benefits to exclusive data, including the ability to make better decisions, improve customer service, and target marketing efforts. And the ability to make special needs pets for vulnerable children to disappear when there's nothing in it for bigger business. However, there are also some risks associated with that, such as the potential for misuse and abuse.

INCLUSIVE DATA

As the world progresses, data also becomes more and more abundant. What was once only available to those with the means to collect it is now available to anyone with an internet connection. This surge in data has led to a new era of exclusive data: data that is only available to certain people or organizations.

This exclusive data is often incredibly valuable, as it can be used to make better decisions, improve products and services, and give businesses a competitive edge. The rise of exclusive data is thus inevitable, as it provides immense value to those who have access to it.

As our world becomes increasingly digitized, the way we collect and store data is changing. And with these changes come new opportunities for marketing and data analytics.

One sure trend that is to continue is the rise of exclusive data, and fall of inclusive data. This is data that is collected by a single organization and also not shared with anyone else. For example, a company might collect data about its customers' purchase history in order to better target them with marketing messages.

Exclusive data can be extremely valuable to organizations because it gives them safety margins. It can also be used to create custom models and algorithms that are specific to the organization's wants and needs.

As exclusive data becomes more common, we can expect to see more companies invest in collecting and storing it. We can also expect to see more innovation around how this data is used to drive business decisions.

The importance of more exclusive data in the future

In the past, data has been collected and used by many different entities in a variety of ways. This has led to some problems, such as data breaches and misuse of information. In the future, it is important that data be more exclusive, so that only those who need it can access it. This will help to protect people's information and privacy.

INCLUSIVE DATA

There are a few ways that data can become more exclusive. One way is for companies to encrypt their data so that only authorized personnel can view it. Another way is for companies to limit the amount of data they collect and store. Finally, companies can develop better policies and procedures for managing their data.

By making data more exclusive, it can help to protect certain people's information and privacy. This is important for exclusive individuals and businesses alike.

Chapter 4

Looking Down Exclusive Data's Barrel

The future of exclusive systemic data

As the world increasingly relies on data to make decisions, the question of who owns this data and how it is used becomes more important. Currently, most data is owned by large corporations who use it to their advantage. However, there are a growing number of individuals and small businesses who are beginning to collect and use data as well. Ultimately, which will out:

large corporations with their unfair advantages or small individuals?

The prophetic David's of data don't stand a chance against the Goliath's of data. Goliath's flood the internet with data that can both erase David's digits and redact Goliath's missteps or David's will to advance the weaker data. It's like Goliath is a huge tsunami and David is a tiny boat in the middle of the ocean.

The data exclusively provided in this article come from reliable sources that have been carefully vetted. The reader can be confident that the information is accurate and trustworthy. Although some of the data may be complex, it has been presented in a clear and concise manner. This article provides an insightful look into the world of data and its potential implications.

It is becoming clear that whoever controls the data, controls the future. That's why it's so important that we ensure that oxygen is accessible to everyone, not just those with deep lungs, before it's too late. That's why it's so important that we ensure that data is accessible to everyone, not just those with deep pockets, before it's too late.

Data is one of the most important aspects of our lives. It helps us make decisions, track progress, and understand the world around us. Without data, we would be lost.

But what happens when data starts to control us? When we become so reliant on it that we can no longer make decisions without consulting a database first? This is the situation we find ourselves in today. We are drowning in data, and it is slowly but surely taking over our lives.

The rest of this book and series of books will explore the dominations and dangers of living in a world where data is king.

The internet is a huge collection of data, or information. Just like a library is a collection of books. And just like it's important for everyone to have access to books at the library, it's important for everyone to have access to data on the internet.

Like Olivia and her mom had an Academic Cavityism in an earlier part of this chapter, a senior who's a friend of mine recently had a Digital Cavityism and a Legal Cavityism. It's like getting a cavity in two teeth that you can't get rid of no matter how much you brush.

The domination and dangers of living in a world where data is king

In a world where data is king, it's easy to feel like you're constantly being watched. Your every move is tracked and monitored, and your personal information is up for sale. It can be hard to keep up with the ever-changing landscape of data privacy and security, and even harder to protect yourself from the dangers that come with it.

There are plenty of dangers that come with living in a world where data is king. Your personal information is constantly at risk of being leaked or hacked, and you're always being tracked and monitored. You might not even realize how much information you're giving away every day.

It's important to be aware of the risks that come with living in a world dominated by data. Stay informed about the latest threats and take steps to protect your personal information.

Legally, one of the saddest, most backward things I've ever seen from two exclusive data curbs was my 70-year-old aunt's false conviction in 2021. A false accusation she lost and was, for a time, held against her because she lost. Now, she did not lose that because she was guilty, there were mountains of physical evidence and witnesses on her side. Plus, mountains of obviously "backwards" evidence on the other. But she was judged against by default because number one, she couldn't afford to buy a lawyer. And number two, because she didn't have access to a computer during an e-hearing and the Coronavirus Pandemic. From her perspective, that's now a gaping hole in two bodies of records like two missing pieces in the puzzle that is her life. It's like finding out that two of your favorite TV shows have been canceled. It's something that can never be replaced and it will always be on her mind.

In conclusion, it is clear that data is becoming increasingly important in today's society. With the rise of technology, and the increasing availability of data, it is becoming more and more difficult to ignore the impact that data has on our lives. Data is collected in a variety of ways, from a variety of sources, and used for a variety of purposes. However, one thing is certain: data is here to stay, and its importance will only continue to grow.

Increase in use by businesses

The future of data exclusive to businesses is looking very bright. Companies are realizing the potential of data and are starting to invest more in collecting and analyzing it. This trend is only going to continue as businesses become more and more competitive and try to get ahead of their rivals.

Like shooting fish in a barrel with no gas pedal or vehicle to take directions, billing customers is easy when you have exclusive tools.

There are a few factors driving this increase in use of data by businesses. Firstly, the amount of data available is increasing at an unprecedented rate thanks to the proliferation of devices and sensors that are constantly connected to the internet. Secondly, advances in artificial intelligence and machine learning are making it possible to extract valuable insights from data that would otherwise be unusable.

Finally, the benefits of using data are becoming more and more apparent as organizations see the impact it can have on their bottom line.

Data has always been a valuable asset to organizations, but its benefits are becoming more and more apparent.

As data becomes more accessible and easier to analyze, organizations are able to make better decisions, faster.

Data-driven decision making has become essential for organizations in all industries in order to stay competitive. Those who can harness the power of data will be able to make better decisions about their products, services, and customers.

The benefits of using data are numerous, but some of the most important include:

-Improved decision making: Data provides organizations with the ability to make informed decisions based on facts and evidence. This allows them to avoid costly mistakes and make decisions that will improve their bottom line.

-Faster decision making: In today's fast-paced world, organizations need to be able to make decisions quickly.

Chapter 5

Data's Developing Hostile Takeover of Vulnerable People for Profit

The data is being used to create floods that target vulnerable people for profit. In particular, data is being used to target low-income people and people of color. This is done by marketing flood insurance to these groups of people and then jacking up the prices when they are the most vulnerable. This practice is known as redlining.

Redlining and redacting both have a long history in the United States. It began in the early 20th century, when insurance companies and banks began using race data as factors in determining who to lend money to and insure. This practice was formalized in the 1930s by the Federal Housing Administration, which created maps that divided cities into "good" and "bad" areas based on race. The "good" areas were white, while the "bad" areas were black.

This practice has continued into the 21st century

A decrease in data use by vulnerable people is when they stop using as much data or the quality of their data usage decreases. This can be due to various reasons but is often due to financial insecurity or other life stressors. While a decrease in data use may not seem like a big deal to some, it can have a very negative impact on vulnerable people. This is because many companies and organizations now rely on big data to make decisions about everything, from what products to sell to where to allocate resources. If vulnerable people are not using as much data, they are at risk of being excluded from these decisions and becoming even more marginalized.

"They say the flood forgets, but those who were flooded remember."

Professionally, another Digital Cavityism curb that many drown under, preventing so many individuals from becoming affluent like taking away their gas pedal or pouring acid in their mind, was when I was at a community center helping a friend apply for a job at Caterpillar. The eager applicant then hit 72 technology, digital and intellectual barriers. It was as if the applicant had run into a wall at full speed, only to find that there were 72 more walls, exactly like the first one, stretched out ahead of them. Literal, digital and psychological obstacles in technology (from his organic perspective) and thus, backward information, backward psychology, and backward software curbs. 72 socioeconomic curbs before he needed ramps before he could turn in a simple job application. These backward-binding curbs of data, otherwise flooding the streets, represent job Application Data Cavityism. And similar reports indicate the more willing an applicant is to try digital job application data, the harder it hits and the worse they fall if it fails to yield applicable results. It's like getting punched in the stomach. The harder you're hit, the worse you feel. Because Application Data Cavityism can affect the human psyche, the digital divide, and the scarce pool of job applicants.

The digital divide is the gap between those who have access to technology and those who do not. The effects of the digital divide are far-reaching and can be seen in many aspects of life. One of the most obvious effects is on the human psyche. When people are constantly exposed to images and messages that they cannot access, it can lead to feelings of frustration, isolation, and even inferiority.

The digital divide has also impacted the job market. With so many people competing for a limited number of jobs, employers can afford to be picky regarding hiring. This often leaves job seekers feeling desperate and hopeless. Additionally, the digital divide creates a scarcity of qualified applicants for many positions. This can make it difficult for employers to find qualified candidates, which can lead to even more frustration and resentment among job seekers.

"The flood forgets, those who were flooded remember, and those who are safe stop."

A decrease in data use by vulnerable people can be seen as a good thing or a bad thing, depending on the perspective.

From a business standpoint, it could be seen as a loss of potential customers and profits. However, from an ethical standpoint, it could be seen as a way to protect people who are at risk of being taken advantage of.

In collaborative times, there are many reasons why someone might want to reduce their data usage. For example, they may be worried about their personal information being collected and sold without their consent. They may also be concerned about targeting ads and other forms of marketing that are based on their data.

Reducing one's data usage can be difficult, but some steps can be taken to minimize the amount of data that is collected about them.

How else is data used to exploit people?

It's no secret that data is big business. Personal data is collected and sold by companies every day, sometimes without the consumer even knowing it. This data can be used to exploit people in many ways.

One way data is used to exploit people is through targeted advertising. Companies use data they have collected about consumers to target them with ads for products and services they are interested in. This can be helpful if you're looking for a new pair of shoes or a new car. But it can also be used to exploit people's weaknesses and vulnerabilities. For example, if someone is struggling with addiction, they may be targeted with ads for alcohol or drugs.

Another way data is used to exploit people is by selling their personal information to third-party companies. Companies may use a person's data to market products and services to that person. They could also sell data about you to banks, insurance companies, or other businesses. The company that sells your data will then try getting you to buy its products or services.

Who is most vulnerable to data exploitation?

In a world where data is increasingly valuable, those who are most vulnerable to data exploitation are also the ones who stand to lose the most. This includes people who are already marginalized or oppressed in some way, as well as children and other vulnerable populations.

Data exploitation can take many forms, from targeted advertising that takes advantage of personal information to outright identity theft. But no matter what form it takes, the result is always the same: someone is taking advantage of another person's vulnerability to make a profit.

On the organic side of screens, there are some ways to protect yourself from data exploitation, but the best defense is always awareness. If you know what you're up against, you're more likely to be able to defend yourself. So if you're concerned about becoming a victim of data exploitation, stay vigilant.

Data's developing hostile takeovers of vulnerable People for profit

It's no secret that data is becoming increasingly important in our world. What is often overlooked is the way that data is being used to take advantage of vulnerable people for profit. This should stop.

Data-driven hostile takeovers are becoming more and more common, and they are often preying on those who are least able to defend themselves. The elderly, the poor, and minorities are all disproportionately targeted by these schemes. And too often, they end up losing their life savings as a result.

This must change. We must put an end to data-driven hostile takeovers before even more people suffer. We must ensure that those who are most vulnerable are protected, and that data is used for good, not for greed.

Without New Data and Organic Data Metrics

Exclusively fundraising Data Cavityisms are occurring across the board. It's raining data backward like acid rain on the brains of those excluded. Whether you work in the medical field or in software applications, people rely on computers, data, and searches to perform various tasks affecting our livelihoods.

Cavityisms occur from the "least" of us to the "greatest" of us. Cavityisms are like colds, they can affect anyone from the weakest to the strongest person. From "least" of use in the morgue and coroner reports after death that publishes the cause of death as quasi-Covid-19 for corporate benefits. It is like saying that the person died of COVID-19, but they're not entirely sure. To the "greatest" of regulators who influence quasi-cause of death, reports befitting the institutional data sometimes funded campaigns. It is like a group of people sitting around a table trying to decide how to best manipulate data to get the most money from the government.

As our reliance on computers, data and search grows, so does the impact these tools have on our lives. From the way we find and consume information, to the way we interact with others, our dependence on technology is evident in many aspects of our daily lives.

While some may view this dependence as a positive, others see it as a negative force that is slowly eroding our ability to think for ourselves and connect with others on a deeper level. In a world where we can find the answer to any question with a simple Google search, are we losing our capacity for critical thinking and independent thought?

Only time will tell how this increased reliance on technology will affect us eventually. For now, it seems clear that it is here to stay and we must learn to adapt accordingly.

Data Cavitysims are occurring from the "right" of us to the "left" of us. It's like we are driving on a freeway and all the cars around us are going in the opposite direction. Should we be concerned about it? Maybe, maybe not. It's hard to say. We'd each must conduct more research on individual circumstances before we could make a definitive statement on it.

However, Inclusive Data is not happening at all. Data metrics can be incredibly inclusive, but this is not happening. Data is instead being used to target vulnerable people for profit. This is unacceptable and must be stopped.

Data can be used to help people in several ways. It can be used to track trends, predict outcomes, and understand complex systems. However, data is not being used for these purposes. Instead, it is being used to target vulnerable people for profit.

This must stop. Data should be used to help people, and unhurt them. We must share that those who have access to data metrics use it responsibly and for the benefit of all, not just a select few.

Don't let data be used to exploit you - be informed, be inclusive, and be safe.

Recently, data has become a commodity. Companies like Facebook and Google have made billions of dollars by collecting data about their users and selling them to advertisers. But data is not just valuable to companies; it can also be used to exploit vulnerable people.

In 2012, the city of Chicago experienced one of the worst floods in its history. The flood was caused by a perfect storm of weather conditions, but it was exacerbated by the city's aging infrastructure and inadequate drainage system. So let's throw some socioeconomic life preservers in the mix with organically Inclusive Data.

Chapter 6

For Healthy & Safe: Inclusive Data Rescue

Fighting and filling cavities organically (Not meant for teeth)

Inclusive Data rescue work is a different way of looking at information and data that's more inclusive of everyone. Especially those with super-special circumstantial, intellectual, and physical needs. Dentists can/t even feel what a tooth cavity feels like to you, but you feel it every moment. It considers the fact that data is often biased and that not everyone has access to it. It is a more democratic, or sub-democratic, way of looking at organic data interventions that can help update the future. It is like a mini democracy "in your mouth" where everyone has a say in what happens and organic data interventions can help guide the future.

Just like democracy has different branches of government that work together to serve the people, your mouth has different types of cells that work together to keep you healthy.

When you need data for your project or a search, you typically can get it from a free online search engine. Like needles in haystacks. They have various data filters and web crawler sets for you to access, including census data, crime data, and more. They want to give all the people access to the data they need. But, are more dental tools better than one?

Inclusive And Exclusive Data

INCLUSIVE DATA

Inclusive data is a more vivid world where inclusion rules and everyone is given an equal voice. This type of data is not exclusive to any one group, search, or person, but is instead open to interpretation by anyone who needs a filling or to fight cavities. Inclusive data can help organizations make softer decisions because it allows for a wider range of perspectives.

Inclusive data is like a beautiful garden that everyone can enjoy. It is full of color and life, and everyone is welcome.

Exclusive data, on the other hand, only included information that supports a single perspective. This type of data can be useful for making quick decisions, but it can also lead to bias and exclusion. Exclusive data often exclude important details that could help people understand the issue at hand.

Imagine that you are trying to escape a haunted house. You come to a fork in the road and see two paths. One path is seen with light and the other path is pitch black.

It's like being in a dark room with only a flashlight to guide you. You can only see what's right in front of you, and you're not sure what is lurking in the shadows.

Inclusive data is a more comprehensive way of understanding the world around us. It includes everyone's voices and perspectives, which can help us make more informed decisions.

Inclusive data is about representing all voices and experiences, not just those that fit a particular narrative. It's about making Data Cavityism history. Data Cavityism is the practice of using data to reinforce existing power structures and narratives. Inclusive Data can help update the future by providing a more accurate representation of the world we live in. Inclusive Data can help improve the efficiency and safety of all operations - inside democracy and out.

Chapter 7

DATA PARADOX

The Prognosis With Open Data Cavityism

Open, infected cavities are a serious problem that can lead to numerous complications. If left untreated, they can cause pain, data infections, and organic data damage to those involved and the surrounding people. In severe cases, it can even lead to an inability to survive.

A Plainfield, Illinois, a family says their 20-year-old student died by suicide after seeing a -$730,000 Robinhood app balance. It's like if you worked really hard to study a trading app and saved a few dollars over the course of two years, and then saw that your bank account balance was suddenly -$730,000. You would naturally feel completely defeated, overwhelmed, and hopeless.

The Prognosis With Open, Infected Financial Cavityism

Since then, the family of Alexander Kearns, who was using an app called Robinhood to trade complex options instruments, has been demanding answers from the millennial-focused trading app (Egan, 2020).

What factors contributed to his death is still a quasi-mystery.

The tragic loss of life has demonstrated the dangers of free-trading. Market experts believe the tragedy is the result of Robinhood's trading app, which may be too alluring to young people who may not understand the risks. First-time information gatherers and potential investors now have easy access to exotic financial instruments typically used by sophisticated investors.

The Kearns family believes Alexander was misled by the app's interface suggesting he owed $730,000, when that was not really the case.

"The kid threw himself in front of a train over nothing, because a tech company can't figure out they shouldn't show a negative $730,000 cash balance to a 20-year-old kid," Bill Brewster, a relative of Kearns, told CNN Business (Egan, 2020).

How much are we thinking about pushing floods of data, and not thinking about the consequence to those floods?

"We are personally devastated by this tragedy," Vlad Tenev and Baiju Bhatt, Robinhood's co-founders and co-CEOs, wrote in a blog post Friday afternoon that confirmed Kearns became a customer. Brewster shared a public post on Twitter that he said Kearns had left before he died, which indicated that he became distraught and confused over his Robinhood account.

"How was a 20-year-old with no income able to get assigned almost a million dollars' worth of leverage?" Kearns replied in the note that Brewster posted (Egan, 2020).

Twitter users who noticed Brewster's thread of tweets alerted him that option buyers on Robinhood occasionally see a negative cash balance until the other half of their trades are executed.

In other words, Kearns may not have actually owed $730,000. But he was apparently led to believe he did. "My sense is that it was all over nothing. It was a user interface issue," said Brewster (Egan, 2020).

Imagine you're a student alone in a dorm room at school. You're online and your cousins, whom you look up to, are all talking about how they're making money by trading options on Robinhood. You're not sure what they're talking about, but you're desperate and it sounds like they're doing something safe with some authority.

The Prognosis With Open Data Cavityism

The prognosis of open, infected cavities in teeth are dependent on how far the infection has advanced and what bacteria are present in the infected tooth. This can best be determined by a literal (not virtual) dental exam.

Open Data Cavityisms are no different. Cavitysm's the common difference between Exclusive and Inclusive Data. It's the name given to the idea that missing data, like any other resource, is scarce and should be literally ultra-safe because it can have levels (or depths) of unnecessary suffering if not. It's like having a cut on your arm. If you leave it untreated, it will become infected and you will eventually experience more pain than if you had just taken care of it in the first place.

The term Data Cavityism was coined by economist William Nordhaus in a paper published in 1974. Nordhaus argued that data should be treated as a public good, like air or water, and that its use should be regulated to prevent its depletion.

Since then, the idea of Inclusive Data scarcity has been widely accepted by economists and policy-makers. But there are several problems with this way of thinking about data.

First, it ignores the fact that data is constantly being created. Each time we use our phones or computers, we generate new data and physiological metrics we sense. This means that the supply of data is not fixed, as Nordhaus assumed. Nor is it non-impactful as some might assume. It's like a cavity in your teeth or that Head & Shoulders commercial with Troy Polamalu. The one where he comes up behind Patrick Mahomes and surprises him. Mahomes asks, "Wait, you work here?" And Polamalu says, "I'm never not working." Polamalu also demonstrates that constant when he becomes a golf coach, car wash attendant, dental hygienist, and actor. In other words, Data Cavityisms, like tooth decay and

Polamalu, never stop working; they literally flood markets and users.

Second, the idea of data flooding leads to a flooded mentality. It's like being caught in a riptide. The water pulls you under and the only thing you can focus on is survival. This means supply warrants an organic valve. It's like drowning in a sea of data, with no end in sight without it. You can see the shoreline getting further and further away, and you start to panic. Knowing now, there are hungry sharks and no hope.

Just like physical flood wipes away everything in its path, so too does data flooding lead to a mental state of chaos and confusion. Those who are caught in the deluge of information are left feeling overwhelmed and unable to process it all.

The Prognosis Caring for Open Data Cavityism

Data (also known as information) is the lifeblood of any organization and family in the modern world, but it's only as good as the people who present, interpret and use it. It is essential for life and health, and must be carefully monitored and managed. Too often, data are siloed within departments and used to support decision-making that benefits only a small group within an organization. Imagine that you're locked in a room with no windows and the only way out is a small door. On the other side of the door is a group of people who are laughing and having a good time. Which eventually becomes a social decay or cavity and is why Cavityism needs to be filled.

This, what we now call, the Deadly Data Paradox, is why it is important to have inclusive data- so that everyone can have a say in what goes on and no one gets excluded. When data is excluded, it can create problems and make things unfair. So let's work together to ensure that Almighty Data Cavityism is history!

Chapter 8

Data Care, Relief and Restoration

Cavityism care, prevention and brimming new data for Granny's sake

Amy is a teenager who lives in Montgomery County, Texas, with her mom. She's the grandchild of a disabled veteran grandmother. Amy spends most of her time alone at home. She grew up watching her grandma receive admiration, esteem, and respect from others. It was like watching a flower bloom in front of her eyes. Not only from grandma's friends talking about their war experiences, but according to her testimonies. Grandma was an elegant speaker. Later in life, after she returned home from the war, grandma was in the business of law. She was famed for her psychological battlefield command. She was a superb divorce lawyer, known for her shrewd and tenacious courtroom tactics.

Amy always heard from her mom that the cases her grandma traded and won at the county courthouse were top-notch. Amy wasn't sure what her mom was talking about, reminiscing about her grandma most of the time, Amy was too young to remember her. Her grandmother died before she was born. But now, Amy was older, desperate to know more. Needing to find her place in the world.

Upon further investigation at the courthouse, it was revealed that grandma wasn't the heroic figure Amy's mom had made her out to be. She lost several times for reasons that were beyond what can be seen now. Researching data was like looking at a snow-covered mountain through a telescope. Amy could see the mountain clearly, but she couldn't see the details of the data like rocks and trees. Her grandma wasn't a hero at all on record and looked to be more like a criminal with scores of losses than esteemed success.

So Amy went to a local attorney nicknamed "Daredevil Dan." That was his nickname because he always went out on a limb despite the evidence in a case and ended trials like Perry Mason. He was the gambler, always betting on the long shot, and sometimes it paid off big time.

Amy was convinced that Daredevil Dan could uncover more information about her grandmother's heroic acts. She wanted to see for herself. What did the world think of her grandmother? After all, everyone had an opinion, and she needed to know if it was good or bad.

Dan asked to see the papers Amy had copied online about her grandma's cases. She couldn't pay him any money, but Dan said he would look into it for free. Amy was shocked and asked why he would do such a thing? He said that if she could find the proof of what data people back then knew, it could make him famous. He will be praised yet again, for being more clever than the clues.

It turns out that Daredevil Dan ended up looking bad. Like stubbing his toe hard. And, in the process, forcing Amy and Amy's mom to misstep. They wasted valuable time and resources just to look bad as well. Dan had never found relief data to support the fact that grandma was a courtroom hero. He combed through old newspapers and dusty archives for weeks, but he never found any evidence that would help him and Amy build a case for grandma's heroism. It's like looking for a needle of data in a haystack.

The ultimate guide to brimming data grandma would love, and the Mom Test would approve

Unlike Daredevil Dan, Angel Ang was a socialite. Her family had owned a restaurant across the street from the courthouse for over 50 years. Amy thought if Ang knew any eye-witness stories about her grandma in court, surely she would share them. She called Ang on one Sunday night. And soon, they were having tea together every day at the family restaurant. They were like two peas in a pod. Ang was always a great guide when it came to making Amy's Grandma-loving and Mom-approved data cared for. Finding her way in the world was no longer like trying to herd cats.

Ang's parents were always very strict with her growing up, so when she started showing an interest in law and happenings at court, they were hesitant. They eventually relented though and allowed her to take some classes at the local community college and watch trials. After a few years of night classes and a few years of observation, Ang earned her degree and passed the bar exam. Yet, she always felt that something was still missing.

While she enjoyed working as a lawyer and being socially active, Ang couldn't believe how boring her life was during her career, without the thrill of partying and doing outrageous things with her friends. But it turns out, she knew people better than most. It's as if she has a sixth sense of understanding people. Angel was pleased to observe the real side of people who came and went from her daily life, not just the judge's side. It was like looking at a Monet painting; from afar it looked like a mess, but up close each brushstroke was beautiful and distinct.

There is no "right" size, or amount of Inclusive Data for New Deals

Remember the story of the little girl with the golden locks who found a house with three bowls of porridge? Remember, when you think about the right amount for Inclusive Data: not too little or meaningless, and not too much or aggressive, but just right! You don't want to have too little data (like the porridge that was too cold), or too much data (like the porridge that was too hot). Your members and special needs benefactors will appreciate your well-played efforts, compelling thoughtfulness, and digit-turning experiences together. When your use of specialized communications skills are both accurate and precise, and your grasp of the talent search is evident, then you have demonstrated a clear understanding of the New Deals, and your participation is both well accepted and appropriate to the search at hand. And when your New Deals are that good, who's counting?

Unlike Daredevil Dan, who was just flippant, Ang always felt in her heart that she was quietly pioneering a new way of looking at data and exchanging records. Discounting systems, she thought, instead of eliminating reality makes sense.

Now today, Amy sits across the table from her, sipping tea. Quietly inkling for the same. Desperately needing to find her place in the world by undiscounting her mom and grandmother. It's like listening to her trying and trying to take the data-stained glasses off her face. Because otherwise, Amy's world is a blur.

After partnering with Daredevil Dan, Amy told Ang, "Was like partnering with a flower wilting right before my eyes." Amy went on, "But partnering with you Ang, is like watching a flower bloom right before my eyes."

Ang confirmed those feelings she's had all along. "Yes, I know! It's like you're forced to pedal harder and harder as the inclining of the trail gets steeper and steeper. The gears on your mountain bike start to feel heavier and heavier, making it even harder to keep going. Yet, it never ends!"

"Exactly," Amy replied. "It's like trying to push a shopping cart up a hill; the higher you go, the harder it is. But chatting with you, who knows everything differently, is like being able to coast once, to get past the blisters on my hands. Finally, being able to avoid some work and being able to see is such a treat."

Daredevil Dan and Angel Ang had two different perspectives on deal-makings and data. Angel feels that Daredevil Dan is too reckless and doesn't think through his deals properly. Daredevil Dan thinks Angel Ang puts too much work into deal-making and data. And, in the middle came Amy. Who just wanted to find out more about her darling grandmother. So Amy and the two attorney's happily agreed to check into New Deals data her friends at the local community center were making, and the results were surprising.

Never before had people with disabilities had such a voice. The team could see like superheroes that other people's lives were opening up and shining like a bountiful treasure chest.

More and more vulnerable people with disabilities feel that they never had a voice until now. They feel that their voices are finally being heard and that they are appreciated for who they are. They see themselves as superheroes because they are finally able to show the world what they're capable of.

When it comes to the size or amount of Inclusive Data for New Deals, there is no "right" answer. It all depends on the situation and what works best for the family or community. Some teams may find that a small amount of data is all they need to get started, while others may need a larger amount. The important thing is to start with what you have and then build from there.

Inclusive Data: How Making Almighty Data Cavityism History Can Update the Future, is data that's open to natural interpretation, like Angel Ang, and used by anyone within any nonprofit organization and family member in need. Read on to discover the best possible brimming new data granny could ask for. It's like having life-saving juice with your deadly donut. You need a side of Inclusive Data.

Chapter 9

Step-by-Step Guide To Dual Data Futures

I. The basics of New Deals Official Intelligence (OI)

Friends. When we think of friends, we think of people we know. With whom we interact regularly. We usually have an idea of who our friends are and how we interact with them. We share common interests and activities and support each other through thick and thin. OI friends are similar, but they exist in the quasi-digital world and their common interests are socioeconomic data ramps and algorithms for the less fortunate. That's organically official and not what others think or talk about our relationships.

Just like human relationships, friendships between OI deals are built on trust. Authentic information is the lifeblood of OI, so sharing it is a big deal. But sharing data also comes with risks. If data is mishandled or misinterpreted, it can lead to serious consequences for the future OI dealings. Like those bad people who say or print bad things about other people on social media.

That's why developing trust is essential to forming friendships in the world of OI. When OI agents know they can trust each other, they're more likely to share data and cooperate on projects. This operation is essential for advances in official intelligence.

Imagine trying to put a puzzle together without having all the pieces. It would be nearly impossible to complete the puzzle and you would get frustrated. The same goes for trying to advance in big data without this second future open top possibilities; it's essential in order to make progress.

Angel Ang was a lawyer who also loved OI and socializing. She found that the two disciplines fed off of each other in ways that gave her insights others couldn't imagine: her legal training helped her to see OI as a missing puzzle piece to be solved, while the physical uplifting of OI helped her to stay sharp and focused in her law practice and community.

"There's a lot of problem-solving in both disciplines," she says. "In OI, you're constantly faced with new obstacles and challenges, and you have to figure out the best way to earn by overcoming them. It's the same in law - you're constantly presented with new problems and challenges, and you have to figure out the best way to solve them."

Ang says that the mental and physical discipline required for OI has helped her to be a better lawyer.

II. Where it could it could break

Organically Advancing New Deals OI Partners With Inclusive Data is a step that discusses the partnership between two nonprofits or family members, New Deal OI and Inclusive Data. These partnerships will help create more inclusive data sets for official intelligence (AI) training and development purposes, but are at the same time custom and unique to each individual's obstacles and achievements in navigating past each obstacle.

Together, we specialize in creating OI un-search engines that eventually "pay our problems away quickly," but exclusive data will always socioeconomically get in the way. Their data sets are always exclusive of overrepresented groups. whereas ours is always inclusive of unrepresented individuals. Like bad apples that say or manufacture bad things about others compared to good friends.

Bad apples are like those friends who are always gossiping and start drama. They're not really bad people, but they can sure ruin a good time. Good friends, on the other hand, are like sweet apples and juicy.

Any new partnership between these two friends will help create data set gardens more representative of the world's population. This is like planting a garden together. You each have your own plot of land, but you share seeds, plants, and tools. By working together, you can create a more diverse and representative garden that will be more enjoyable for everyone. This is important because it will help ensure that official intelligence authors are trained on data reflecting the diversity of the world.

This partnership is part of New Deal OI's commitment to advancing social justice through know-ability, authenticity, and technology.

Daredevil Dan was a lawyer who almost despised OI and loved AI. OI, he assumed, is the practice of analyzing data to find new business opportunities. AI, or artificial intelligence, is the practice of using computers to automate tasks that would traditionally be done by humans.

Dan found that OI required a lot of time and effort to sift through and include data that was often uncomfortable, unstructured and messy. It was tedious work that didn't always yield results. On the other hand, artificial intelligence could quickly process large amounts of data and identify patterns that humans might miss.

For Dan, the choice was clear: he would rather spend his time on something that was more lucrative no matter the results. That's why he decided to focus on AI instead of OI.

III. Instead, dual data is like developing a sustainable business

Regarding OI, sustainability has a few different meanings. For one, there's the need to ensure that an OI friend can keep practicing without outside systemic intervention – what's known as "family" un-sustainability in the name of "family sustainability." There's also the question of whether an OI margin will have long-term social and economic benefits for everyone involved – what we might call "ethical nonprofit sustainability." The two different meanings of sustainability are like trying to maintain a healthy diet. You can eat junk food every once in a while, but if you want to be sustainable, you must ensure most of what you put into your search is nutritious.

Healthy family sustainability is important for two reasons. First, if a mom wants to use OI to automate some of her child-rearing concerns, she needs to be confident that the search will keep working or growing even as the data and circumstances change over time. Second, a sustainable knowledge base is more likely to be used and trusted by others and communities alike. Ethical sustainability is key to ensuring that these families and organizations can continue to provide crucial margins to those who need them.

In a world where big data is increasingly becoming the norm, it's refreshing to see the OI community taking the steps necessary to ensure that families and those with special needs remain at the center of the process.

When Daredevil Dan started losing cases in court and respect on the streets, he didn't understand how to save his practice. Fortunately, his friend Angel and her partners knew exactly what to do. Their New Deals, profit margins and growing respect showed Daredevil Dan how to use his time for the activities that most mattered in terms of building a sustainable practice.

IV. Picking the "Goldilocks margins" of data

Regarding data, the Goldilocks principle applies that too little organic data results in inaccurate models, while too much-processed data can lead to overfitting. Like a team of doctors may overdiagnose a patient if they are presented with too much unnecessary data. The key is to find the perfect amount of dual data that results in the most accurate at-home model for payable solutions possible.

This is especially important when working with official intelligence (OI), as the goal is to create algorithms that accurately represent the real world. To do this, OI needs access to large amounts of data care. However, simply having a lot of data care is not enough – the data care must be high quality and diverse to create an accurate, rewarding network.

The Goldilocks margin can help organizations and families strike the perfect balance when it comes to their data and balancing value to it. By ensuring that they have just the right amount of high-quality data, they can create OI balances that are more accurate and reflective of reality. The Goldilocks principle refers to the idea that something needs to be just right, or in the case of OI, just the right amount.

The idea behind the Goldilocks principle is that when it comes to data care, everything should be "just right".

V. Do you have it just right?

Regarding "just right" data care, there are a few key things to keep in mind if you want to make sure you have the right deal for OI. First, the deal (or communicative collaboration) should be of high quality and inclusive of as many peer situations as possible. This might sound foreign at first. But keep in mind, it takes a team to keep any family together. Especially when no one thinks or communicates in the same way.

Second, it should be well-organized and accessible so that OI can easily learn as it develops. In other words, OI "ramps" built should have a space near you and their counterparts' screens where they can easily access all of their previous collaboration data. This could be done by searching Google while accessing ReboundGo on another tab. Or digitally signing an agreement while accessing rewards through ReboundGo in your space too.

Third, it should be adaptive. Because the nature of OI is constantly changing, their deal will update and change as should yours with it.

Finally, it should be endlessly up-to-date. We'll need to ensure that programmers have the right licenses and permissions in place so that everyone can use the data and rewards for "just right" OI purposes.

If you can check off all of these boxes, then you're likely on the right track regarding securing data for OI and unsearches where you need to "earn problems away quickly."

However, it's also important to keep in mind that data is constantly changing and evolving, so even if you have the perfect data set today, it's important to stay on top of trends and update your advancement (or balancing acts) regularly.

VI. Do you have it "just right" in your organization or family?

Regarding data, all organizations and all families are not the same. Nonprofits are very competitive as far as applying for funding or seeking political favor. Organizations and families, therefore, are often at odds with each other or have conflicting focuses. Organizations want clean data, concise, and easy to interpret. Families, on the other hand, often have messy, unorganized data that can be difficult to decipher. This disconnect can lead to tension and conflict between the two groups.

To avoid this conflict, it is important for organizations to partner with inclusive data providers who can help them understand and use the family's data. By working with an inclusive data provider, organizations can get the information they need while also respecting the family's privacy and preferences. Inclusive data providers can also help families understand how their data is being used and ensure that it is being used in a way that benefits them.

VII. Introduce a successful pilot deal

Regarding creating a successful pilot deal, there are a few key things to keep in mind. Primarily, it's important to be inclusive of data when making any decisions. This data should come from various sources, including customer feedback and market research. Additionally, it's important to have a clear understanding of what you're trying to achieve with the pilot deal. What are your goals and objectives? What are the risks and the potential rewards? By taking the time to answer these questions upfront, you will be in a much better position to negotiate a successful pilot deal.

VIII. Adopting a Journey from Catityism to Talentism (C2T)

This can be a special project like needing to call a taxi to go to the doctor but living alone and no longer being able to see. C2T (Cativityism to Talentism) is a journey that begins with the recognition that all people have an inherent value and should be treated with dignity and respect. A push of a button or a home visit gets the journey started. This leads to the realization that everyone has unique talents and abilities that must be nurtured and developed. It is only through the unlocking of these talents and abilities that we can create a world that is truly inclusive, adaptable, and equitable for all. Calling a cab when you can't see is hard inside a closet, but un-marginalized your-their journey with Talentism ain't. What other journeys will you profit from?

C2T is about moving away from a system that relies on a few select individuals being in charge, to one where everyone has a role to play. It is about moving away from a system where some people are seen as more valuable than others, to one where everyone is valued for their unique contributions.

We are still on this journey, and there is much work to be done, but C2T proves us a roadmap for how to get there. I'd like the finishing line to be like a quote from Nelson Mandela, which I think is a fitting way to end: "A good head and a good heart are always a formidable combination." That's what next-generation leaders are standing on!

IX. Leading with C2T

To create more opportunities for people of all backgrounds, New Deal OI has innovated Inclusive Data. These partners and benefactors will help New Deal OI to better understand the needs of underrepresented communities and design products and services that meet their specific needs.

Inclusive Data is a social enterprise that collects, cleans, and analyzes data from underrepresented groups. They use these data to help businesses make more informed decisions about product development, marketing, and sales. By working with Inclusive Data, New Deals AI will be able to tap into a wealth of knowledge about the experiences and perspectives of people who are often overlooked by the mainstream tech industry.

This partnership is part of New Deal OI's larger commitment to advancing social justice through technology. By collaborating with Inclusive Data, they hope to create products and services that are truly inclusive and accessible to everyone.

X. Reach maturity

Regarding data, the adage "the more, the merrier" definitely applies. The more data that's available for official intelligence (OI) algorithms to learn from, the better those algorithms can become at completing specific tasks. But gathering enough data to train OI can be difficult and expensive. That's why many companies are now turning to synthetic data: computer-generated data that mimic real-world data sets. Which isn't organic, but interesting nonetheless.

One company that's been particularly successful with synthetic data is Life Winks. Life Winks is a "synthetic data" platform that transforms raw data into more manageable data sets usable by software developers and business analysts. Along the way, Life Winks also helps families or companies serving families improve the accuracy of their algorithms, making their bottom line better for tasks like credit scoring, fraud detection, and victim-proof discoveries.

Other successful startups use AI to help businesses automate their customer service processes. To train its AI algorithms, corporate AI systems generate millions of synthetic customer service conversations. These conversations are then used to teach the AI how to handle real customer service inquiries. Example: Drift uses AI to offer live chat, email, and voice call support for businesses. The company's machine learning algorithms automatically respond to customer queries based on the information that a customer enters the chat window.

XI. Absorb New OI Partners OR Just old AI deals?

As your organization or family seeks to increase official intelligence (OI), you may be debating whether it is better to build new partnerships or capitalize on existing ones. There are advantages and disadvantages to both these approaches.

Building new partnerships can help you gain access to innovative technologies and data sources that can provide you with a competitive edge. However, developing these relationships takes time and resources. You may also have to make significant investments upfront without knowing if the partnership will be successful.

If you choose to pursue existing AI relationships, you may be able to more quickly achieve results. These relationships also come with built-in trust and understanding, which can save time and money. However, you may not have as much control over the direction of the relationship, and you may not be able to take advantage of the latest advances in AI technology.

To be more inclusive, ReboundHeros have partnered with Inclusive Data. This partnership will help the future better understand and address the needs of their friends. The Inclusive Data platform will function with anonymous, but valuable data about their friends, which will help them to make informed decisions about how to best support their family or members. It is about data care, instead of data floods.

XII. Refresh with glowing reviews

As OI and its Organic Inclusive Data Garden continue to grow, it is important to remember the importance of inclusion and highly exclusive data floods. Inclusive data helps ensure that everyone has a voice in the search or decisions being made about the future of its users and heroes. Without careful inclusive data, it is easy for severely excluded people to be excluded, forgotten, or worse, flooded without care.

The OI from organic C2T has been successful in part because it has been able to gather rewarding data from a wide variety of experiences. This has allowed it to help make more valuable searches and more informed decisions about the best way for the most voiceless to move forward. However, they have not always been successful in including everyone in their search and decision-making process.

There have been times when certain groups have been excluded from the conversation altogether. This can lead to a feeling like one's concerns are not being heard or that their voice doesn't matter. Over time, as the probabilities of achievements navigating past obstacles become more customized organically, the data will tip back in favor of people, and less in favor of open flood gates.

INCLUSIVE DATA

Finally, to partner augment exclusive systemic data profits with Inclusive Data profitability, visit and download the free Starter Guide.

Chapter 10

Un-Marginalizing Data Ramps

All-natural organic data care and escalation deals

Organic data care is the term given to the new era of data collection, management, access, and analysis that is currently underway. This shift is being driven by advances in technology, the need for customized personal development, and a growing awareness of the need for more ethical and sustainable approaches to data. A world in which data is consistently used to help people live healthier, happier lives.

The solution to hostile data was all-natural organic data care. It's the inherent part of Inclusive Data. This is a new type of data care that is sweeping the nation. It is revolutionizing the way we care for our data. It is an all-natural, organic way to keep our data healthy and safe. But, that's not enough for everyone. Because curbs need ramps for our transportation- and mobility-challenged community.

Organic data care ramps (and hero partner rampers) rely on the principles of inclusion, transparency, and co-consensual profitability. It recognizes that true data care is a shared resource that belongs to all of us and that it should be managed in a way that benefits everyone equally. This means collecting only the necessary data, keeping it safe and secure, and ensuring that people have not just access to systemic data when they need it, but co-authorship when transformation's needed.

Imagine you are a doctor trying to diagnose a first-time patient, but didn't have access to their medical records when you needed them. Not because you and the patient were not together in a room. But because they could not speak or author information and all previous authors of records were nowhere in sight.

Co-authorship is like two people working on a painting together. Whereas Inclusive Data are having access to other vivid, industry standards of data other doctors and patients practice in particular cases.

By having access to New Deals, other doctors' and patients' data can be transformed. They'll get a better sense of what industry standard transformations are out there. This, in turn, can help others improve their own lives or practice.

Therapeutically Improving Data

If you want your data to be truly cared for, the solution is all-natural organic data care. This type of care goes beyond just ensuring your data is backed up and secured. It also means taking proactive steps to ensure your data is healthy and growing. Here are some tips for systemic data care:

1. Keep your data clean by regularly deleting old files and junk mail. This will help keep your system running smoothly and prevent problems caused by clutter.

2. Keep your software up to date with the latest security patches and updates.

Here are some tips for all-natural, organic data care:

1. Keep your information local. Just as you would with food or medicine, keeping your data in a safe plain in your mind near you will help it stay top-of-mind, fresh, and relevant.

2. When possible, use handy communication devices. These tools such as a voice recorder, pencil, and paper

or Braille writer are non-exclusive and won't affect the quality of your data.

3. Avoid using hostile outside data or marketing commercials in thoughts about your data storage devices. Again, just as you would any other type of food or medicine, bad food or medicine can damage delicate data areas of your psychology and render them useless or misinformation.

4. Be sure to handle your data with open people and avoid contaminating the thoughts from other sources.

A simple analogy to all-natural data care is hygiene or personal grooming. Just as you wouldn't want to keep your dirty, unkempt beard for too long, so is it with your data. Letting your data become unkempt and neglected can lead to serious problems down the road.

The organic data care movement is still in its early stages, but it is already making a significant impact. Numerous peers are beginning to adopt these principles, and more are sure to follow suit in the years ahead.

If you're concerned about the harsh information in "your" data or data acquisition sources, you're not alone. Many people are looking for natural and organic solutions that won't harm their future. Luckily, there are plenty of all-natural and organic data care options available. From unsearch "search" engine washes to comfort ramps, there's an all-natural option for every step of your life-care routine. Not only are these safer private networks (SPNs) safer for your life when special needs arise, but they're also better for the community. So why not make the switch to Inclusive Data care today?

But if you're concerned about systemic Data Cavityism and the future of "your" data, as far as Inclusive Date being unwillingly purged, many people are using more concrete transformative data called Talentism. Talentism is the practice of using your data to transform your life in a way that makes you more competitive. This data can be used for any number of reasons, from improving your health to finding a better job to helping you reach your financial goals. A "Journey with Talentism" world in which those with the most cared-for data are the most successful too.

Chapter 11

Talentism: Real-World A-OI

Using real-world artificial and official intelligence (A-OI) data nexus develops a New Deals knowledge base and relives or redresses hostile exclusive data barriers with Inclusive Data care

Talentism is a term that was coined by Dr. Thomas Armstrong to describe a new way of looking at intelligence. It is based on the premise that there is more to intelligence than what can be measured by IQ tests.

Armstrong argues that we need to start valuing talents and abilities that are not traditionally considered intelligent, such as creativity, musical ability, and athletic ability. He believes that these talents are just as important as IQ in predicting success in life.

Talentism is an important concept because it challenges the traditional view of intelligence and reminds us that there are many different types of intelligence. It also highlights the importance of giving everyone an opportunity to succeed, regardless of their IQ score.

The origins of Talentism

In the early 21st century, the world economy shifted from one based on natural resources to one based on human resources. This new era, which some have called the "knowledge economy," has placed a premium on creativity, innovation, and "thinking outside the box." As a result, talent has become the most important commodity in the global marketplace.

The idea of talentism—the prioritization of talent over all other factors in economic development—was first proposed by economists Richard Florida and Charles Murray in their 2002 book The Rise of the Creative Class. They argued that traditional economic indicators like gross domestic product (GDP) fail to capture the importance of creativity and innovation in driving economic growth.

Talentism has been embraced by many cities and regions as a way to attract and retain top talent. These cities and regions are often referred to as "talent magnets" or as "world-class cities.

How Talentism manifests in the real world

In the real world, Talentism manifests itself in a number of ways. First, it creates a meritocracy, where the most talented individuals are rewarded with the best opportunities. This can lead to a situation where the less talented are left behind, as they are not given the same opportunities to succeed. Additionally, Talentism can lead to a situation where those who are born into talent or have access to better resources are more likely to succeed than those who do not. Finally, Talentism can create an environment where only the most talented individuals are valued, and everyone else is considered expendable. This can lead to a lot of pressure on those who are considered "talented," and can ultimately be harmful to both them and society as a whole.

The benefits of Talentism

In a rapidly changing world, those who succeed will be the ones who are able to adapt. To do this, organizations must embrace what is known as "talentism." Talentism is the belief that the best way to achieve success is by investing in and developing the talent of individuals. This means creating an environment where people can do their best work and providing them with the resources they need to grow and develop.

There are numerous benefits of Talentism. First, it leads to improved organizational performance. When organizations invest in their employees, they are more likely to retain them and see an increase in productivity. Second, it helps businesses attract top talent. By creating a culture of development and opportunity, businesses can attract the best and brightest employees. Finally, it fosters innovation and creativity.

The drawbacks of Talentism

While talentism has certainly contributed to the success of many individuals, there are also a number of drawbacks associated with this way of thinking. For one, talentism can lead to a sense of entitlement and narcissism. When people believe that they are simply born with talent and that this is what sets them apart from others, they can become arrogant and dismissive of those who don't have the same gifts. Additionally, talentism can foster an environment of competition and comparison, rather than cooperation and collaboration. When everyone is focused on being the best, it can be difficult to work together for the common good. Finally, talentism can create pressure and stress, as people feel like they have to live up to their talents and perform at a high level all the time. This can be detrimental to both mental and physical health.

When it comes to addressing the real-world A-OI, talentism provides a way for individuals to identify their strengths and weaknesses and determine how best to use their talents. However, it is important to remember that no one is perfect and that everyone has different strengths and weaknesses. The key is to find a balance between using your talents to achieve your goals and being open to learning new things.

Ultimately, Talentism can help you achieve success in the real world by providing a framework for identifying your strengths and weaknesses. However, it is important to remember that no one is perfect and that everyone has different strengths and weaknesses. The key is to find a balance between using your talents to achieve your goals and being open to learning new things.

Organic Talentism as a bridge to systemic interface issues relief

There's no doubt that data is becoming increasingly important in our lives. It helps us make better decisions, understand the world around us, and even find new friends. But as data becomes more and more ubiquitous, it's important to ensure that it's inclusive of everyone.

So how can we make data care inclusive? First, we must ensure that data is collected from a wide variety of sources. In this way, we can be sure that the data reflect the richness and diversity of our world. Second, we must ensure that data is accessible to everyone. This means making it available in different languages and formats so that everyone can use it. Finally, we must ensure that data is used for good and that Official Intelligence (OI) is never left off the table. This means using it to help solve problems like poverty, hunger, and disease for all.

It's like using a hammer to build a house. You can use it to build something amazing that will help people, or you can use it to smash projects and hurt people. It all depends on how you use it. But leaving a hammer out of the process of building a home is not good judgment. It's like trying to bake a cake without flour. Sure, you can add sugar, eggs, butter, and vanilla extract, but your cake is never going to come out right without the flour.

Inclusive Data is data that includes everyone. Especially if that means to defy being excluded. It’s not just for the chosen few or the 1%. It’s for everyone. And it’s about time we had some. Making Almighty Data Cavityism history can update the future because when we have Inclusive Data, we can make better decisions. We can see what’s working and what isn’t. We can see who is being left behind and why. And most importantly, we can see better to do something about it.

We can identify areas where people are struggling and offer targeted assistance. Which is like seeing someone carrying a heavy load, and can tell they're struggling, so you offer innovative ways to help them carry it.

We can see which groups of people are being left behind and design programs to help them.

We can monitor progress over time to ensure that no one is left behind.

We can find out why more and more people are struggling and address the root causes.

In conclusion, organic data care is the term given to the new era of data collection, management, access, and analysis that is currently underway. This shift is being driven by advances in technology and growing awareness. The benefits of organic data care include improved data quality, better customer insights, and more efficient decision-making. Especially when that means solidifying talent. Like taping a hammer in your hand during the process of making a checklist of various tools you need to build a house, putting the sugar in the bowl beforehand prevents you from forgetting about it in the future, putting together a puzzle with all the pieces included, and performing at-home work in your search does not leave out the important digits.

Chapter 12

Inclusive Data's Future

Inclusive Data care is the future. It's time to move beyond the "data bias" that has plagued our world for too long. Inclusive data is about making data more representative of the world we live in, and it's something we should all be striving for.

Everyone has numerous reasons why Inclusive Data is so important. For one, it helps us have a better life and make more informed life choices. When data is more representative of the world around you, you can more accurately understand trends and patterns. It allows us to make more informed decisions that impact everyone equally.

Secondly, Inclusive Data may be like reaching for the stars and so not always be considered achievable. Where no one has ever had the opportunity to touch the stars, but the individual effort is well worth it. It can't always benefit every solution that will come about in the future, but in the end, leading to a search with open access is beneficial. One that future generations will remember.

Third, inclusive data promote fairness and equality. Currently, many groups are underrepresented in data sets simply because they haven't been traditionally included. This often leads to disparities in how different groups are treated. By starting and keeping our data organically inclusive, we can ensure that everyone is given the same opportunities from now on. Let's look at an example to see how this works in practice.

INCLUSIVE DATA

In the near future, data will be more inclusive than it is today. By this, we mean that data will be collected from a wider range of sources, including from people who are not currently considered “data experts”. This shift will be driven by advances in technology, which will make it easier to collect and analyze data.

This is a good thing! Inclusive Data will help us to better understand the world around us and make better decisions. However, since we are talking about data in a more inclusive context, then it is important that we also talk about ethics. Since it will be easier to collect and analyze data, the amount of data on the planet will increase drastically.

In the past, data was used to divide people into categories and create hierarchies. This has led to a system where some people are considered more valuable than others and have more opportunities as a result. However, this isn't fair nor representative of the world we live in.

Much has been said about the importance of all data in recent years. But there is reason to be optimistic about the future of inclusive data. In order to achieve this, we need to make sure that the data is representative of all people, and not just the ones who are well-off. This can be done through a number of means. One example is by collecting data in person. Another example is by collecting data from a diverse set of people. This can be done by targeting specific populations, or by making sure that everyone is included in the data collection process. We will also need to improve our methods for aggregating data. But even more vital than that is connecting the dots between research and policy. We need to make sure that policymakers are aware of the findings from scientific research, and that researchers know what policy-makers need from their work.

Inclusive Data, from the other perspective, is data that includes everyone, regardless of who they are or what they look like. It's about creating opportunities for everyone, not just a select few. This type of data is important because it leads to better decision making and more accurate representation.

It's also important because it allows us to see the world as it actually is, not as we want or expect it to be. It means that we can see the good and bad in our society and make decisions that help everyone. This is why I believe that the best way to make data more inclusive is to get more people involved in data collection. It's not just about increasing diversity but about expanding our perspectives and adding new insights. As a result, we can all move forward together rather than apart. #InclusiveDataIsBeautiful

Chapter 13

The Age of Data Breaches, Dark Web, and Free Misuse of Information

The past decade has seen a proliferation of data breaches, with sensitive information like credit card numbers and Social Security numbers being leaked regularly. At the same time, the dark web has become a haven for criminals to buy and sell this stolen data. And if that wasn't enough, there are now numerous ways for someone to get your personal information for free simply by misusing it.

All of this has led to a perfect storm of sorts when it comes to our personal information. It's never been easier for criminals to get their hands on our sensitive data, and once they have it, there's very little we can do to stop them from using it for nefarious purposes.

Imagine a princess who has to save her kingdom from an evil sorcerer who is using people's personal information to control them. That's where I see us today. The princess is on our mobile devices, and the evil sorcerer is using our personal information to benefit us. However, some people don't a princess like everyone else. They are left out of benefits and even the basic protects or safeguards from adversarial misuse of data.

The age of data breaches, the dark web, and free misuse of information has led to a new era of control. In this era, we are in control of our mobile devices and the evil forces that seek to misuse our information. We can protect ourselves and our loved ones by using strong passwords, two-factor authentication, and other security measures. However, we must remain vigilant and be aware of the dangers that exist in this new age.

If you're concerned about your personal information being compromised, there are some steps you can take to protect yourself.

Data Breaches: Describe how data breaches have become more common, and list some notable examples as they come up. Data breaches have become more common in recent years, as the dark web and other free online resources have made it easier for hackers to obtain sensitive information. Notable examples of data breaches include the 2017 Equifax breach, in which hackers obtained the personal information of over 140 million people, and the 2018 Marriott breach, in which hackers accessed the personal information of over 500 million people. Data breaches can have devastating consequences for both individuals and organizations, as they can lead to identity theft, financial loss, and damage to reputations.

The internet has drastically changed the way we live and operate on a day-to-day basis. It has also created new opportunities for criminals to exploit our personal information. In recent years, there has been a surge in data breaches, dark web activity, and free misuse of information. This has led to many people feeling concerned about their online security and privacy. In this article, we will explore the age of data breaches, the dark web, and the free misuse of information. We will also provide some tips on how you can protect yourself from these threats.

The dark web is a place where stolen data is often sold. This data can include everything from personal information to corporate secrets. The dark web makes it easy for criminals to find buyers for this stolen data. This makes it very difficult for companies and individuals to keep their information safe. In the age of data breaches, the dark web is a major concern.

Data breaches are becoming more and more common. In the age of the internet, it is easier than ever for hackers to get ahold of sensitive information. The dark web is full of information that can be used to exploit people and businesses.

The age we live in is the age of data breaches, the dark web, and the free misuse of information. Our every move is tracked and stored by corporations, governments, and other institutions. And often, these entities don't do a very good job of keeping our information safe. As a result, our data is constantly being leaked, sold, or simply stolen in massive data breaches. Meanwhile, the dark web provides a place for criminals to buy and sell this stolen data. And to top it all off, there's an entire industry of companies that profit from the free misuse of our information.

In conclusion, the dark web and data breaches are real and present a danger to the average person. The best defense against this is to be aware of the risks and take steps to protect yourself. This includes being careful about what information you share online and using strong passwords for your accounts. And for those without a princess or basic access, then Inclusive Data is a must. It will help families, nonprofit providers, and partners to process, manage and make sense of special needs socioeconomic data ramp applications. Make sure you protect your data by using Inclusive Data.

Chapter 14

Data of the Future

Data is the new oil. This term is often used to describe the value that data has in today's economy. Just as oil was a key resource in the Industrial Revolution, data is playing a similar role in our digital age. Data is being collected and used to drive decision-making in businesses, governments, and society as a whole.

The term "data of the future" refers to the idea that data will become even more important in the years to come. We are already seeing this play out with the rise of artificial intelligence (AI) and machine learning. As AI gets better at understanding and using data, its impact will only grow. The future of data is likely to be defined by ever-increasing quantities of data and ever-more powerful AI tools.

In the past, data was collected and then stored in a physical location, like a filing cabinet. Today, data is collected and stored electronically, making it easier to access and use. In the future, data will be collected and used in new ways. It will be collected using new technology, like sensors, and used to create new products and services. This data will be used to improve our lives in ways we can't even imagine.

Data is big, fast, and connected. The future of data is even bigger, faster, and more connected. Data is the lifeblood of the digital economy, and it is only going to get bigger and more important in the years to come.

The future of data is big, fast, and connected. Data is the lifeblood of the digital economy, and it is only going to get bigger and more important in the years to come. The world's biggest companies are all racing to build ever-larger databases and develop ever-more sophisticated algorithms for extracting value from all that data. And as our devices become ever more interconnected—via the Internet of Things—the volume of data generated each day will only continue to spiral upward.

Data privacy and security are two of the most important issues facing our society today. With the advent of the internet and the proliferation of personal devices, our lives are more interconnected than ever before. This increased connectivity has led to a corresponding increase in the amount of data being collected about us daily.

This data can be used to track our movements, habits, and even our thoughts. While this data can be used for good (for example, to target ads or improve products), it also poses a serious threat to our privacy and security. Hackers can use this data to target us for identity theft, fraud, or even physical attacks.

The solution to this problem is not simple. We need to find a way to balance the need for data with the need for privacy and security.

Data analytics has the potential to revolutionize the way businesses operate. By analyzing large data sets, businesses can gain insights into trends and patterns that would otherwise be hidden. This information can be used to make better decisions, improve operations, and ultimately boost profits.

Several factors are driving the growth of data analytics. First, the amount of data being generated is increasing exponentially. This is due to the proliferation of digital devices and sensors, as well as the rise of social media and other online activities. Second, advances in computing power and storage capacity have made it possible to process and store this data. Finally, there are now a variety of powerful analytical tools available to make sense of all this data.

The benefits of data analytics are clear. But some challenges need to be addressed. One is ensuring that the data is accurate and complete.

In the age of big data, businesses are looking for ways to harness its power to better understand their customers and predict their behavior. One way they're doing this is through data personalization.

Data personalization is the process of using data to create a personalized experience for the customer. This could be something as simple as showing them relevant products based on their past purchases or providing them with customized recommendations.

Studies have shown that personalization can have a significant impact on customer behavior. In one study, Amazon found that personalized recommendations led to a 29% increase in sales. And in another study, Netflix found that users who received personalized recommendations were 10% more likely to continue using the service than those who didn't.

There are many factors that businesses need to consider when personalizing data, including the customer's past behavior, demographics, and even psychological traits.

The future of data is looking extremely bright. With the development of new technologies, we are now able to collect and process data faster than ever before. This has led to a boom in the field of data science, as more and more companies are looking to harness the power of data to improve their businesses.

The future looks particularly promising for predictive analytics. By using historical data, predictive analytics can provide insights into what might happen in the future. This can be used to make better business decisions, such as which products to develop or how to price them.

The data revolution is coming. Scientists and businesses are already collecting more data than ever before, and they are only going to continue to do so. This data can be used to improve our understanding of the world and make better decisions.

Data is going to change the way we live. It will help us make better decisions, both as individuals and as a society. We need to be prepared for this change.

Chapter 15

Inclusive Data, Options, Margins, Deals & Light

Inclusive Data, Inclusive Options & Deals is an article about how important it is for Users to be transparent with their data and give Users a variety of options to choose from. It can be difficult for customers to trust companies that do not share information openly, so being inclusive with data can help build trust. This type of transparency also allows customers to feel like they are getting the best possible deal, which can lead to repeat business.

In our current digital age, data is power. Inclusive Data allows Users to make better-informed decisions, optimize their searches and services, and ultimately serve their peer universe better. However, not all data is created equal. Inclusive data—data that reflects the diversity of our society—is critical to ensuring that everyone has a fair shot at success.

What are the social benefits of Inclusive Data?

There are many social benefits to Inclusive Data. One of the most important is that it helps to create a level playing field for all users. By providing data that is accessible to everyone, it helps to ensure that everyone has the same opportunities to access and use information. This can help to reduce inequality and create a more fair and just society.

In addition, Inclusive Data can also help to promote social cohesion and understanding. By bringing people together from different backgrounds and providing them with data that they can all use, it can help to break down barriers between groups. This can lead to increased cooperation and collaboration, as well as a greater understanding of different perspectives.

Ultimately, Inclusive Data can help to create a better world for everyone. Ensuring that everyone has access to information, can help to empower individuals and communities.

How can those marginalized use Inclusive Data to their advantage?

Inclusive Data can help marginalized groups to their advantage. By collecting and analyzing data that is representative of all people, businesses and organizations can make better decisions that improve outcomes for everyone.

This is especially important for marginalized groups who are often left out of decision-making processes. Inclusive data can help ensure that their voices are heard and that they have a seat at the table.

Unliberated Blindness

Mary was an experienced traveler. However, she was blind and had many bad experiences being given wrong directions and bad information that set her back. She grew up on the East Coast in the mid-1800s. But before the twentieth century, only a handful of blind people had the chance to become truly liberated (Day).

Blind people have lived in every nation and era, representing every stratum of society. Yet, only a handful of blind men and women had the chance to become literate like Mary, so the vast majority had no way to record their lives for posterity.

Even for Mary L. Day, one of the rare exceptions, life never had much light. One physician called in to treat

Mary on her darkest day and promised to restore her sight. Each attempt by the doctors resulted in failure and disappointment, and most of the treatments were agonizing. The final doctor before she stop going to doctors "directed me to be kept in a dark room for four weeks, with bread and molasses as diet" Mary said. She nearly died (Day) after trial. Needless to say, Mary never felt like risking it all to travel again.

The endless loss of independence

Blindness can be a difficult thing to grapple with. The loss of independence can be one of the most frustrating parts. Having to rely on others for help with the simplest tasks can be maddening and dangerous.

For those who have never had to deal with blindness, it is hard to understand how debilitating it can be. Imagine not being able to see your loved ones' faces, or the sunset, or your own hands. Or to take a pink pill instead of a white pill. It is a loss that is not just hard to put into words, but often backward to your health to try.

Some are born blind, and others lose their sight later in life. Regardless of when it happens, it is always a shock. There is an adjustment period where one has to learn how to do things all over again. Everything from cooking and cleaning, to getting around and reading Braille takes time and practice.

The challenges of daily life

Blindness can make everyday tasks difficult, and sometimes even impossible. Even something as simple as getting out of bed in the morning can be a challenge when you can't see where you're going.

But it's not just the physical challenges that can be difficult to deal with. Blindness can also make it hard to socialize and connect with others. When you can't see people's faces, it can be hard to read their emotions, which can make communicating difficult.

But despite all the challenges that come with blindness, there are also many ways to overcome them. With the right support and attitude, anything is possible.

The lack of employment opportunities

Despite all the talk about jobless economic recoveries, the lack of employment opportunities is very real for many Americans. The combination of long-term unemployment and a shrinking job market has had a devastating effect on workers' ability to find jobs.

In particular, the number of job openings has declined sharply since the recession began. In 2009, there were an average of six job seekers for every opening; by 2016, that ratio had increased to more than 16 to 1. And although the economy has added jobs in recent years, those gains have not been enough to keep up with population growth. As a result, there are still millions of Americans who are unemployed or underemployed.

The situation is especially dire for workers who have been out of work for a long time. Their skills and experience atrophy, making them less attractive to employers.

The social stigma

The social stigma of blindness is a long-standing problem that continues to this day. Though there have been many advances in the treatment and prevention of blindness, the social stigma surrounding it remains. This stigma can be traced back to ancient times when blindness was seen as a punishment from the gods. In more recent history, the social stigma of blindness has been perpetuated by myths and misconceptions about what it means to be blind.

Today, there are approximately 1.3 million people in the United States who are blind or visually impaired. Of those, only about 10% are legally blind. Despite these numbers, the social stigma of blindness persists. People who are blind or visually impaired often face discrimination in employment, housing, education, and other areas of life. They may also be seen as less capable than their sighted counterparts and be treated accordingly.

Blindness can be seen as a metaphor for the lack of knowledge or understanding. Just as a person who is blind cannot see, someone who is uneducated or uninformed cannot comprehend what is happening around them. In both cases, the individual is at a disadvantage and unable to participate fully in the world.

An ignorant person is not necessarily evil, but they are limited in their ability to make decisions and take action. They are reliant on others to tell them what to do and how to think. This can be dangerous, especially if those in power are manipulating the information that is being shared.

It's important to question everything and not take things at face value. By expanding our horizons and learning new things, we can prevent ourselves from being controlled by those who would keep us in the dark.

Expected light for those without special needs

There are many ways that families and organizations can search for information and collect Inclusive Data. This includes surveying a diverse range of people, using demographic data from reliable sources, and conducting focus groups with different stakeholders.

Once this data is collected, it's usually easy to analyze carefully to identify patterns and trends that are healthful. This will allow businesses and organizations to develop policies and programs that match and are more effective at meeting the needs of all people.

What are some examples of the marginalized using Inclusive Data ramps?

There are many examples of the marginalized using inclusive data ramps. One example is when people with disabilities use them to access public buildings. This gives them the independence to enter and exit the building without having to rely on someone else. Another example is when parents use ramps to push strollers up curbs. This makes it easier for them to get around with their children and helps them feel included in their community.

In a world filled with data, options, margins, deals, and light, it can be hard to feel included. But feeling included is an important part of life. When we feel included, we feel like we belong. We feel like we matter.

Inclusive Data, Options, Margins, Deals & Light is an important step toward feeling included. This article will explore what it means to feel included and how to create an inclusive environment for everyone.

How can those with special access needs use Inclusive Data ramps to their advantage?

Inclusive Data is designed to help those with special access needs use data to their advantage. The transformations provide data ramps that can be used to identify opportunities and make better decisions. The ramps provide access to data that would otherwise be inaccessible, making it possible for users to get the most out of their data. In addition, the site offers discounts and deals on data products and services, making it an affordable option for those with special access needs.

Inclusive data, options, margins, deals, and light are all important aspects of society. They help all people make informed decisions, to find new opportunities, and to understand their peer access better. By understanding these things, we can function more efficiently and effectively. We can all experience different levels of light depending on our Inclusive Data needs.

Inclusive Data, Options, Margins, Deals & Light is also about the importance of Inclusive Data and options in the business. It inherently argues against no socioeconomic data ramps for those with special needs that should be inclusive and easy to access for all employees and data users, regardless of position or seniority. They also assert that businesses should give employees more options when it comes to career development and benefits. Ultimately, the goal is to create a more productive and happier workplace through Inclusive Data.

References

Burke, M. (2018, October 17). *Molly Burke on what it's like to go blind.* YouTube. Retrieved September 27, 2022, from https://www.youtube.com/watch?v=GQ34CB1Xd1Q

Day, M. L. (n.d.). *Incidents in the Life of a Blind Girl.* Incidents in the life of a blind girl. Retrieved September 27, 2022, from https://nfb.org/sites/default/files/images/nfb/publications/fr/fr30/2/fr300203.htm

Dempsey, G. (2019, April 25). Cary man died by suicide in McHenry Jail Cell: Source. Crystal Lake-Cary, IL

Patch. Retrieved September 16, 2022, from https://patch.com/illinois/crystallake/cary-man-committed-suicide-mchenry-jail-cell-source

Egan, M. (2020, June 20). Apparent suicide by 20-year-old Robinhood trader who saw a negative $730,000 balance prompts app to make changes. CNN. Retrieved September 16, 2022, from https://www.cnn.com/2020/06/19/business/robinhood-suicide-alex-kearns/index.html

Head & shoulders super bowl 2022 TV spot, 'never not working: Royal oils' featuring Troy Polamalu, Patrick Mahomes. iSpot.tv | Realtime TV Advertising Performance Measurement. (n.d.). Retrieved September 16, 2022, from https://www.ispot.tv/ad/qotp/head-and-shoulders-supre-bowl-2022-never-not-working-royal-oils-featuring-troy-polamalu-patrick-maho

House, P. (2014, August 28). What people cured of blindness see. The New Yorker. Retrieved September 27, 2022, from https://www.newyorker.com/tech/annals-of-technology/people-cured-blindness-see

Poncumhak, P., Saengsuwan, J., & Amatachaya, S. (2014, July). Ability of walking without a walking device in patients with spinal cord injury as determined using data from functional tests. The journal of spinal cord medicine. Retrieved September 27, 2022, from https://www.ncbi.nlm.nih.gov/pmc/articles/PMC4116722/

U.S. Department of Health and Human Services. (n.d.). Project prakash enlightens our understanding of Vision. National Eye Institute. Retrieved September 27, 2022, from https://www.nei.nih.gov/about/goals-and-accomplishments/nei-research-initiatives/international-vision-research/project-prakash-enlightens-our-understanding-vision

INCLUSIVE DATA

GLOSSARY

Almighty Data Cavityism - There is a problem in the field of statistical analysis known as "Almighty Data Cavityism," or "Almighty Missing Data." This refers to the fact that the knowledge about what happened to the missing data is not always available due to counter-gains. Some data metrics profit-making haystacks and not for finding needles in them. In some circumstances, competitors may purposefully disclose erroneous or missing information to their rivals for business, in which case sometimes this happened unintentionally. In other cases, the data may have been deliberately removed to make the results of the analysis more favorable.

AI - Artificial intelligence (AI) is intelligence demonstrated by robots, instead of the superior intelligence exhibited by animals like people. AI research is commonly referred to as the study of meaning-rich agents and knowledge banks, which refers to any network that perceives its ecosystem and takes actions that achieve desirable objectives.

A-OI - is the application of how organic situational circumstances can interface with artificial intelligence systems, in order to create more intelligent data. It's like giving your computer a brain transplant. Artificial and official intelligence (A-OI) is the nexus, from the organic side "of screens," between real people and real performances, transformed psychologies, physiologies, or socioeconomics. It is believed that by bringing these two together differently, we can create a more efficient and effective way of dealing with the vast amount of data that exists today. There are many benefits to this approach, including the ability to speed up decision making, improve accuracy, economically ramp those with special needs, and increase transparency.

Big Data - In computing, big data means extremely large data sets that may be analyzed computationally to reveal patterns, trends, and associations, especially relating to human behavior and interactions.

C2T Theory - The Cavity and Talentism Theory (C2T Theory) is a new scientific hypothesis that suggests that victimhood litigation cavities may be un-linkable to organically documenting hidden talents. The theory is based on the observation that many children with abilities or talents also have case cavities like divorce or parental disabilities and nuclear family gaps when their parents' lives diverge. Physiological gaps between children and their mothers and/or fathers, the theory suggests, cause more serious cavities and organic data leads to more organic talents. It's like trying to fill a hole in a bucket with water. The gaps between the children and their parents are like the holes in the bucket, and the water represents the cavities. Whereas Inclusive Data transforms the missing parts of the bucket.

Corporate Data Floods - The term "corporate data floods" refers to the large amounts of data that corporations generate daily. This data can come from a variety of sources, including customer transactions, internal operations, and even employee communications. While this data can be immensely valuable to businesses, it can also be very difficult to manage and analyze. As a result, many companies are struggling to keep up with the deluge of data.

Data Care - Thought to be extinct for the most part, data care refers to Inclusive Data and its application to all humanity through the augmented use of computers, specifically the internet and other electronic searches. Data care is a term that refers to the human empathy factor with which data is updated and/or added to a quasi-database.

Data Flooded - The recent deluge of people's data has been overwhelming for many organizations. They simply haven't had the time or resources to effectively process and analyze all of this information. As a result, they're struggling to make sense of it all and draw actionable insights. It's a full-time job and resource-rich tracking and cleaning your data from corporate stakeholders and data brokers. This is an understandable challenge that many nonprofits and families are facing every second. However, it's important to remember that this information can be incredibly valuable.

Data Garden - A Data Garden is a community of people who work together to manage and grow data organically. The community works together to identify and track data, ensure that it is of high quality, and make it available to others. The community also works together to ramp up the data when needed and protect the data from being misused or lost.

Data Paradox - Data mining is the process of extracting hidden patterns from large data sets. However, sometimes these hidden patterns can be contradictory, or paradoxical. For example, consider a data set of student test scores. A data miner might find a hidden pattern that students who study more tend to get lower grades. This seems paradoxical at first glance, but it may be because students who study more are also taking harder classes. The Data Paradox can also occur when two seemingly contradictory patterns both exist in the dataset but are just different views of the same underlying phenomenon. For example, a data set might show that there is a positive correlation between smoking and longevity.

Data Ramps - A socioeconomic data ramp is a quasi-computer-generated simulation of real-world conditions that can be used to include social interactions and test vetted economic deals and make partner decisions. The term "ramp" refers to the gradual decrease in complexity as more data is added. Data ramps are useful for special needs access, equality, inclusion, and making the Data Cavityism history with a user self-development market. They can also be used to test different ReboundHero partner scenarios and predict the effects of the proposed New Deals.

Data Ramps disclaimer: While socioeconomic data ramps are valuable platforms to accessibility, they are imperfect. One limitation is that they only simulate conditions that are known at the time the model is created. This means that unforeseen events, such as natural disasters or new technological breakthroughs, cannot be accounted for. Additionally, ramps only provide a limited amount of information about how an economy and social circumstances work; they cannot capture all the nuances and complexities of real-world socioeconomics.

Inclusive Data - Inclusive data is data that includes all relevant access and organic information to make an informed decision. This type of data considers all perspectives and growers involved to provide a comprehensive view of the issue at hand. Inclusive Data is essential for making accessible, well-informed life flows and decisions that consider all potential abilities, impacts, and outcomes.

New Deals - The original New Deal was a series of economic programs implemented in the US during the 1930s in response to the Great Depression. They included public works projects, financial reforms, and regulations aimed at curbing monopoly power. One little-known aspect of the old New Deal was that it lacked special consideration for people with special needs, who more and more today require digital data care. The new New Deal in this book refers to helping the forgotten recover from (and make history) the Great Data Cavityism. And since games like search engine profiteering are for the survival of the financially fittest, ReboundHero, ReboundGo, and ReboundHero.org all offer different knowledge networks of data to counterbalance the odds. Considering the foundational inclusion or point-of-need profitable information in additional data before (and at) the point of trauma. What if trauma-induced people could have fitting assistance through adversarial post-event trial-making debates, follow-up trials, and concrete decisional data? Would post-trauma be minimized or prevented?

New Deals Data Gardens - New Deals Data Gardens are a type of data care quasi-storage network that allows users and heroes to access and share authentic friendships in a secure ecology. A flourishing of information is now used by nonprofits with special needs and families with special needs to access custom and customizable validated data. The New Deals Data Garden collaboration is designed to provide users and heroic partners with the ability to access and share data safely and securely. This network provides users with the ability to control who has access to their barriers and how those barriers are discounted.

OI — OI, in this book, refers to intelligence that is regarded as official intelligence (OI). Think of OI as the co-captain of the Inclusive Data ship. In OI, the vetted and validated shared intelligence that is exhibited is not typically considered in corporate settings, artificial intelligence (AI), and artificial intelligence research. Instead of overwhelming intelligence exhibited by robots and robot-rich data, OI more commonly refers to the socioeconomic intelligence of friendships and Family as Policy. In other words, it is the ability to address People differently, respectfully, and to solidify their socioeconomic developments as complementary to AI. It is like being able to speak to different people in different ways, respecting their backgrounds and cultures, and working together to improve everyone's lives.

Organic Inclusive New Deals Data Gardens -
Friend-building friendships and family-building Family

enables self-adaptive algorithms to network custom socioeconomic data escalators. Transforming data and redefining accessibility, for those with super-special circumstantial, intellectual, and/or physical needs. Imagine that you are in a wheelchair and want to go to the top of a very tall building. There is an elevator, but it is out of order. Inclusive Data helps you flourish by staying on the ground.

ReboundHero - Partnering with the ReboundHero project offers a unique service to family members and nonprofits to help people with special needs directly. The impacted data care then self-develops beyond those circumstances. Our organic algorithms are custom-groomed to create socioeconomic data escalators that redefine accessibility for our partners, heroes, and users. This enables them to live more independently and reach their full potential. Our service is particularly beneficial for those who have super-special circumstantial, intellectual, or physical needs. We are committed to helping our clients overcome any obstacles they may face and in the most profitable talents possible.

ReboundGo - If you're looking for a fun and easy way to make some extra cash, look no further than ReboundGo! With this unique unsearch engine app (disguised as a search engine), "We-pay-you" to quasi-access the internet for the things you're already interested in. (Qualifications, Terms, and conditions apply). Not only is it a great way to earn some extra money, but it's also a great way to distract and pay yourself for earning your everyday problems away. So why not give ReboundGo a try? (Disclaimer as of 2022: ReboundGo is a self-developing smartphone app and computer app).

Safer Private Network (SPN) - The term "underground railroad" typically refers to a network of people and places that were used to help slaves escape from the American South to freedom in the Northern states or Canada. In this context, the term SPN for the launch of Inclusive Data in the form of Constructive Child Safety

Files in 2011 is being used to refer to information that is essential for human survival. The design of the old binding filing systems, data from high-conflict divorce psychological warfare operations, onset of disability cases, and deployments to war, are such that people can be identified by the two-party adversarial data and data metrics they do not have access to, but no middle ground. The design of the old binding filing systems was highly inefficient and often resulted in data being lost or misplaced. The data from high-conflict divorce psychological warfare is often used as a way to manipulate and control the other party and third parties. This can be highly damaging to the individuals, and can often lead to further conflict and violence. Even though the risks of two fighting parties wrecking each other are plain to see and feel for third parties, risky data and even riskier data metrics are obvious and expected. For victimhood survival, denied systemic representation for those who can't afford counsel, an expensive retainer fee or a college degree is common to play. This is not what a truly open network, freedom, representation for all, and Constitutional Rights should do, and therefore this secret is more about the SPN for Inclusive Data.

Afterword

In the early 1900s, a few people in the know felt like they were forced to organize to protect children from the free exploitation of then-legal child labor. In the early 2000s, a few of us in the know felt like we were forced to organize and start our SPN (underground safer private network) to protect our special needs children from exploitation by legal, unregulated, adversarial litigation and exclusive maneuvers. United CLU parents programs help unrepresented parents with unrepresented children by advocating for organic constructiveness in case cavities and also time and money lapses in missing family connections kids have to carry. A reuniting ministry for excessively hollowed-out nuclear family gaps and the likes, socially, emotionally, financially, psychologically, and physiologically.

Prior to co-founding our freedom-centric CLU group, I had experienced a lot of hardships in my life. Like many of us, I'm sure, I was the child of a divorce and an adult of a high-conflict divorce with no relief in sight and now my children are not able to . I also suffered broken dreams with the onset of a disability. I have a background in engineering and knew that data and data-collection metrics were different for engineers than for divorce/disability contracting systems. They're corporately malpractice to each other. So I decided to re-imagine helping people who are going through the same things I did.

Learning from is all, now, like many of us, I'm an un-litigator, an un-attorney, an un-lawyer, a systemic "failure" in society. I know those are both taxing and expensive ways. I believe that what we do matters and nothing can stop teams from making a cool $ and cooler differently - so let's learn, understand, and work together naturally on new paths!

Never hurt again safeguarding you and your member's dreams with organic intellectual property (IP) before it's systemically "profitable," while making Cavityism history, paddling your own canoe , your own wallet, unflooding "your" own search operations, and rescuing "your" own self-developing engine .

ReboundGo!

@PracticeBigPracticeSmall

@FloodingLivesSavingLives

About Author

Safeguard your dreams!

Being Least Commanded (Matthew 5:19) has always been an unfair advantage for my colleagues and me, and an "unfair" advantage for systems that hold fast to making labels above us all. We love uncovering the hidden data which is always glossed over a little or glossed over a lot with other adversarial places.

- Hi, I'm Aaron Wemple. Least Commanded author and the founder of Life Winks LLC. I never asked for this, and would rather pray for my shortcomings than talk about myself, but now I love transforming dreams, victim-proofing files & filling in missing organic data ramps, talents, and laws for those with special needs. I also project manage private data metrics for the united CLU parents group and the Future of Data Challenge ReboundHero project. I am best known for following Jesus despite all others, inventing constructive Child Safety Files, which were designed for industrial strength to help divorced or separated parents keep their children ultra-safe during high-conflict adversarial compulsions, and for co-parenting two very intelligent and very talented kids. I am passionate about helping families in need and nonprofits that strive to make a difference in the lives of those who are struggling. I believe that every family deserves to be happy and ultra-safe, and I will continue to work hard to make this a reality for as many disadvantaged heroes as possible.

- I'm partially disabled now, but I previously worked as Facility Administrator at Old Kings Orchard Community Center, TV Director at Maranatha Church,

Electrical Designer with GSI, and sheet metal tradesman with Local 36. My academic study includes a bachelor spanning engineering and psychology from SIU-E, Organizational Leadership at Millikin University, and Electrical Engineering at SIU-E. I work with Paraquad in St Louis, The Family Cafe in Florida, and other ability groups to try and regain some sense of independence.

In recent years, my partners in data and I've been recognized by several news leaders, book reviewers, and government organizations for childhood, family, and community-building efforts – 2020 KPLR-TV/YouTube "Morning Blend" interview with Producer James Thomas; 2019 WAND-TV News "Spring Into Action;" 2018 WAND-TV News "Cleaning Up the Book of Justice;" 2017 WAND-TV News "Clean Child Support Initiative; " 2020 Amazon book and university-lead project "Law & Side-Law."

So now I love ensuring good family performance data stays together organically and partnering with license and data development specialists who are interested in the purpose of "twinning greatness" for special needs people socially. We do this to prevent trauma through our proprietary #NewDeals #PracticingSmall and #SavingLives.

Yes, there are floods and curbs, and life can be a pain, but safeguard your dreams and journey with Talentism anyway. Because everything twins greatness!

Acknowledgments

I'm grateful beyond measure to concur with the benevolent Lord Jesus above all. There is One who is good and then everyone else, including me, trying unsuccessfully to block him. It's like if there is a race and he always wins or if there is a game and he always gets the high score. By literally trying in life I've thankfully lost and thankfully found everything by following Jesus. I lost my way and I've found God anew. I like to remember that every time I reset my thinking, it's like starting over again. "In the Beginning was the Word, and the Word was with God, and the Word was God" (John 1:1). It's like when you're learning to ride a bike, and you fall down. You have to get back on the bike and try again. And again, and again, until you finally learn how to ride without falling down. Resetting your thinking is like that - you have to keep trying until you finally learn how to do it without making too many mistakes.

Thanks to the united CLU parents, family trial support and encouragement group, the Ephesians 4:13 develops and hosts a free online forum where meetings, available for people, with help in overcoming case cavities and other complex challenges facing the family. It is often difficult when families cannot afford to spend money on legal counsel at trial or in the onset of disability and disengagement.

Thanks to my favorite Bible verse, "Jesus said I am the way, the truth and life, no one comes to the Father except through me," John 14:6.

I'm so thankful for my family, friends, Decatur Cares Rescue Ministries "Water Street Mission" Homeless

Shelter, Maranatha Church, Maranatha Church TV Ministry, Decatur, IL Township, Old Kings Orchard Community Center, WAND-TV News, and many others in the Central Illinois community.

I owe a great deal of thanks to BALSA, The Future of Data Challenge, Sheet Metal Workers Local 36, Sheet Metal Workers Local 218, SIU-E, Millikin University, Paraquad in St Louis, SSI Ticket to Work Program, and The Family Cafe in Florida, KPLR-TV "Morning Blend" in St. Louis, Amazon, KDP, Amazon Authors, all of which have helped me try and regain some sense of independence after several physical, socioeconomic and counter psychological severance issues.

And through the concrete twisting and dreary world, with all my failed attempts, content in finding solace and guidance by emulating those who have found similar success by emulating Lord Jesus.

Also By

Inclusive Academics

Inclusive Case: How Making Almighty Case Cavityism History Can Help Us Live A Better Life

Inclusive Data

Inclusive Faithfinder

Inclusive Player: ReboundHero - Never Hurt Again Making Player Cavityism History

Inclusive Psychologies

Inclusive Sociologies

INCLUSIVE DATA

Inclusive Political

Law & Side-Law

Parenting 2.0 For Un-Haters

Regarding Data Cavityism prevention, relief and restoration in this series, please watch for more organic profitability measures and cutting-edge, much healthier safety standards in a number of other spaces of missing OI as well.

This series of books reveals the bigger picture of the changes in lives induced by the original New Deal and the New Deals of today. This simplified method and now series explains these changes to regular families and nonprofits (or industries) in an easily understandable way, making it ideal for those who wish to understand how the world now operates on all-natural pivotal data (or scales), smarter, and safer for everyone.

Made in the USA
Monee, IL
04 November 2026

67378729R00105